"You shall not kill" or "You shall not murder"?

"You shall not kill" or "You shall not murder"?

The Assault on a Biblical Text

Wilma Ann Bailey

A Michael Glazier Book

LITURGICAL PRESS
Collegeville, Minnesota

www.litpress.org

Cover design by Joachim Rhoades, O.S.B.

1	2	3	4	5	6	7	8	9

Library of Congress Cataloging-in-Publication Data

Bailey, Wilma A.
      "You shall not kill" or "You shall not murder"? : the assault on a biblical
text / Wilma Ann Bailey.
          p.   cm.
      "A Michael Glazier book."
      Summary: "In regard to the Ten Commandments, focuses on the change in
the wording of the translations of Exodus 20:13 and Deuteronomy 5:17, from
'kill' to 'murder'"—Provided by publisher.
      Includes bibliographical references and index.
      ISBN-13: 978-0-8146-5214-5 (pbk. : alk. paper)
      ISBN-10: 0-8146-5214-X
          1. Ten commandments—Murder.   2.Bible. O.T. Exodus XX, 13—Translating.   3. Bible. O.T. Deuteronomy V, 17—Translating.   I. Title.

BV4680.B35 2005
222'.1605208—dc22

                                                                            2005001213

Contents

Preface

Sometime in the middle of the twentieth century a subtle, often over-looked change occurred in the wording of a biblical text. The sixth commandment,[1] "You shall not kill" (Exod 20:13) became "You shall not murder" in many, and certainly the most influential, English Bible translations. Often the stated reason for the change is either "The Hebrew word used in Exodus 20:13 means murder everywhere in the Bible" or "In other texts, killing is permitted and sanctioned by God; therefore this commandment cannot be understood as a general prohibition against killing." The first of these statements is not correct. The Hebrew word does not mean murder everywhere, as Chapter One will demonstrate. The second statement can also be proven faulty, though perhaps not false. Unfortunately, there is no absolutely objective way to interpret Scripture. Humans are shaped by such factors as their environments, their place in history, their culture, their families, their economic security or lack thereof, and their personal and political commitments. These factors come into play even for translators who are striving for the most accurate translation possible and for interpreters who are trying to be faithful to the text. For example, in Judges 20:18-28 it appears that God is giving the Israelites permission to fight against and therefore kill Benjaminites (one of their own tribes). But the Israelites lose the battle (twice)! How is this to be interpreted? Was God sanctioning war in the minds of the Israelites? Was God demonstrating that war is not the way to go, that it only leads to self-destruction? The Israelites ask God again. God tells them to fight. This time they win, but one Israelite tribe is nearly exterminated. Is this a sanctioning of war and killing, or is this to

[1] In the Roman Catholic Church and the Lutheran Church the "You shall not kill" commandment is counted as the fifth commandment.

be read in light of the critique at the end of the book of Judges: "Every person was doing what was right in their own eyes" (translation mine). So even texts that appear to sanction killing may, in fact, be doing the opposite.

The sixth commandment is perhaps the most disturbing of all the commandments. This is evidenced by the lengths to which scholars and church folk go to explain it away. Most killing throughout history has taken place within the context of what is legal (e.g., war, capital punishment) and therefore exempt from this commandment in the minds of many people. Interpreters narrow the prohibition to what relatively few people do, a criminal act—a person illegally killing another person—while allowing for the bulk of killing that takes place in the world to continue.

This commandment exposes the true moral substance or vacuity of its interpreters. The Quaker Elton Trueblood once observed: "The ultimate moral principles of a people are revealed, not by what they *do* but by the way in which they defend their actions."[2] This book will not focus on theological interpretation as such, though the implications of the textual change for theology and particularly ethics are significant, but on the meaning of the Hebrew word used in Exod 20:13 and the altering of the English translation of the commandment in several large traditions during the twentieth and twenty-first centuries.

The four tradition streams examined in this book are American forms of Evangelical Protestantism, Mainline Protestantism, Judaism, and Roman Catholicism. Because these are broad tradition streams, statements made about them will not fit every denomination (or individual) generally categorized within that tradition. Most notably, the Peace Churches as a collection—the Mennonites, various Brethren groups, and the Quakers—though they all oppose killing even by legal authorities, do not easily fit in any of the categories. Moreover, this study examines the question of how Bible translations have treated the sixth commandment, and the Peace Churches have not produced Bible translations of their own. Most Brethren churches consider themselves to be evangelicals. Many Mennonites also consider themselves to be evangelicals, though some streams of that tradition do not fit an evangelical mold, particularly as that term was understood in the second half of the twentieth century. Quakers (more properly Friends) fit in neither the evangelical nor

---

[2] Elton Trueblood, *Foundations For Reconstruction* (rev. ed. New York: Harper & Brothers, 1961) 61–62.

the mainline category. The term "mainline" itself does not represent theological commonality, but the place of the denomination in American society. The Roman Catholic Church, the largest of the Christian churches, has an official voice that represents it and has produced its own Bible translations. Judaism is not strictly defined by religion. Jews are a people, a community. Whether religious or not, Jews have a common tradition of ethical teachings. The Eastern rite churches are omitted from this study because they have not as yet produced their own English Bible translations.

Special thanks are due to Dr. Walter Harrelson, who read the first chapter and offered helpful suggestions, critique, and memories of the conversations surrounding the sixth commandment in the NRSV committee. Thanks to Lorna Shoemaker, director of the CTS Library, for locating a number of sources for me, to attorney William J. Holwager for help with legal terminology, to Pastor Jane Sims of the Pentecostal Assemblies of the World for sharing her memories of pacifism in that denomination and the movement away from that stance, to Fr. Francis Bryan of Marian College for elucidating the term "counsel of perfection," to Dr. Liana Lupas of the American Bible Society and John F. Rathe of the New York Public Library for locating a hard-to-find source and sending the information to me by e-mail, to Martha Yoder Maust for reading two chapters of the manuscript and offering helpful suggestions, and to Rabbi Dennis Sasso for unintentionally giving me the idea to write on this topic. I particularly want to thank Linda M. Maloney of the Liturgical Press for carefully reading and critiquing the entire manuscript. Special thanks are offered to the Christian Theological Seminary for granting a research leave during which a first draft of this manuscript was written. And to everyone past and present who contributed in large and small ways to the understanding of the sixth commandment, "Thank you!"

Chapter 1

"You shall not kill"*

It is indeed ironic that during the century that might be described accurately as the most violent in the history of humankind to date, with its relentless assaults on human persons, witnessed in the slaughter of 167 to 175 million people in what Zbiginew Brzezinski incisively describes as "politically motivated carnage,"[1] in addition to the killing of millions by handguns, assault rifles, knives, clubs, weaponized tools, bare hands, preventable accidents or illnesses, policies and programs that slowly extinguished the very lives of the poor and vulnerable around the world, almost every major English Bible translation:[2]—the *TANAKH* (1962), the *New American Standard Version* (1971), the *New International Version* (1978), The New King James Version (1982), the *New Revised Standard Version* (1989), and the *Revised English Bible* (1989)—changed the wording of the sixth commandment from "You shall not kill" to the more limited "You shall not murder," granting, in the minds of many, biblical permission for the mayhem to continue. Why did this happen? What was the

---

* Another version of this chapter appeared as an article in *Encounter*, vol. 65, Winter 2004, no. 1, pp. 39–54.

[1] Zbigniew Brzezinski, *Out of Control: Global Turmoil on the Eve of the Twenty-First Century* (New York: Scribner, 1993) 17.

[2] The *New American Bible* (1970) and the *New Jerusalem Bible* (1985) are the only ones to maintain the translation "You shall not kill," in solidarity with the older Tyndale-Coverdale (1535), Geneva (1560), the *Authorized* or "King James" *Version* (1611), Douay-Rheims (1609–1610), the *English Revised Version* (1901), and the *Revised Standard Version* (1952).

motivation of the translators who were involved in this semantic shift? Which English word represents the better translation of the Hebrew word used in Exod 20:13: "kill," or "murder"? What does it say? What does it mean? Why does it matter? This book will examine this significant change and what it will mean to future generations whose ethical understanding of the commandment stops short of a prohibition against killing.

This first chapter will argue that the English word "murder" is too limited and too varied a legal term to function adequately as the translation for the Hebrew word *rtsḥ*,[3] that the use of *rtsḥ* in other biblical texts indicates that the word is meant to be translated more broadly, that the verbal form of *rtsḥ* often appears in a list or an ambiguous phrase that makes it impossible to determine a precise meaning, and that murder is too rare a crime to merit Ten Commandment status.

Translation Is Not Easy

Translation is a complicated business. It attempts to bridge a gap not only between two languages, but between two cultures. In the case of biblical languages there is another gap, a separation between historical time periods. Words that emerged in an ancient rural village culture of the East are being translated into the language of a postmodern urban culture of the West. In some cases there is no word or phrase in the first language that has the same meaning in the language into which the word or phrase is being translated. For example, if you are a speaker of English and you want to translate the word "ice" into a language spoken by people living in a tropical rainforest, how would you do it, if the people in the rainforest had no word for "ice" in their own language? You might focus on what it is about ice that you want to emphasize, such as its color, its texture, its coldness, or its ability to melt as the temperature changes, and choose a corresponding word that represents that quality. But you will not find a word that conveys all the qualities at once in the language of the targeted audience. If it had all the same qualities, it would be the same thing. Consequently, the people who live in that tropical rainforest will only be able to get a limited understanding of

---

[3] The root letters of the verb are presented here and throughout the book so that non-specialists may follow the argument. Hebrew readers may turn to Appendix 2 for the specific form of the word.

what you mean. Even when there is a corresponding word in a language, the words may be understood differently because of cultural or environmental differences. The word "dog," for example, may conjure up a different set of images in a society where dogs are used as work animals, or eaten for dinner, than in a society where dogs are pets. You can translate the word, but it will be understood differently by the intended audience. A further complication is that the meanings of words can change over time even in the same language. In the early seventeenth century, when the King James Bible was translated, the word "conversation" meant "conduct" or "social interaction," not the act of talking, but behavior.[4]

When the art of alphabetic writing was invented in the ancient Near East it functioned primarily as a mnemonic device or for record-keeping. The reader (meaning a specialist who read aloud to others) was expected to fill in the gaps and contextualize the story or announcement. In the case of the Bible we do not have that authoritative reader, and our location does not share the physical environment, cultural, social, economic, or historical contexts of the text. In the case of the words "kill" and "murder" two primary languages are involved. One is Biblical Hebrew, the language of the Hebrew Bible.[5] It is over two thousand years old. The other is English, specifically late-twentieth-century American English, the language of the translations that are most commonly used in the churches of the early twenty-first century.

What Is the Difference Between "kill" and "murder"?

We begin by defining the words in question: the English words "kill" and "murder," and the Hebrew word that appears in the "You shall not kill" commandment (Exod 20:13), *rtsh (ratsoah)*.[6]

The *Oxford English Dictionary*, taking into consideration both British and American English usage, defines murder as "the unlawful killing of a human being with malice aforethought; often more explicitly willful murder."[7] Unlawful means that legal killings (war, capital punishment,

---

[4] "Conversation," s.v., *The Oxford English Dictionary* (Oxford: Oxford University Press, 1989).

[5] Christians call this collection the "Old Testament." Jews call it the "Tanakh."

[6] This is the infinitive form of the word. The word appears in several different forms. In Exod 20:13 it has a second masculine singular imperfect (prefix) form.

[7] *Oxford English Dictionary* (2nd ed. Oxford: Clarendon Press, 1989) 10:107.

self-defense, and in some jurisdictions euthanasia, suicide, etc.) are not murder. As long as the act of killing is approved by a legal entity, it is not murder. Notice that the *Oxford English Dictionary*'s definition of murder also requires that the state of mind of the killer be taken into consideration. If the killer intends harm prior to committing the act that resulted in the death of another, the act is murder. This is the definition of the venerable *Oxford English Dictionary,* but it is not adequate. Why? Because the word "murder' is a legal term. As such, its meaning varies from one jurisdiction to another.

In the United States murder is defined in the legal code of each individual state, and it varies from state to state. The Oxford Dictionary definition most closely resembles the definition of murder found in the California Penal Code, which reads, "Murder is the unlawful killing of a human being or a fetus, with malice aforethought."[8] However, in the state of Indiana the definition of murder is "A person [sic] who knowingly or intentionally kills another human being."[9] Importantly, the Indiana Penal Code does not require that the killing be unlawful, nor is the state of mind of the killer taken into consideration—no malice aforethought. The person needs only to intend to kill. Self-defense therefore may be labeled murder in Indiana, but not in California. In Pennsylvania a person need not kill anyone at all to commit murder. If a person is killed in the course of committing a crime that is a felony, both the killer and the accomplice are guilty of murder.[10] There are people serving natural life sentences in Pennsylvania under this definition of murder. They never killed or intended to kill anyone, but their partner in crime did. This raises the issue of whether a word that is understood differently by readers in different locations is the best choice for a Bible translation that is meant to cross state and national boundaries.[11] More will be said about this in the last chapter.

[8] California Penal Code #187, at www.law.cornell.edu/topics/state_statutes2.html.

[9] Office of Code Revision, Indiana Legislative Services Agency, 1C35-42-1-1, at www.law.cornell.edu/topics/state_statutes2.html.

[10] Pennsylvania Consolidated Statutes, Crimes and Offenses (Title 18), Part 2: Definition of Specific Offenses #2502. Murder. http://members.aol.com/StatutesPA/18.Cp.25.html.

[11] This was an issue when a revision of the King James Version was undertaken by British and American scholars in the late nineteenth century. British definitions and word usage were different enough that Americans decided to create their own version with American words and phrases. The latter version was the *American Standard Version,* the former the *English Revised Version.*

Unlike murder, "kill" is a common word with broad implications. The definition of "kill" that will be used follows the *Oxford English Dictionary*'s second definition which is "to deprive of life,"[12] with the assumption that a human is being deprived of life (though this need not be the case in English).

The Hebrew word *rtsh* is defined as both "kill" and "murder" in standard lexicons.[13] In the Even-Shoshan Hebrew concordance *rtsh* is defined using another Hebrew word, הרג (*hrg, harog*), which also means "kill," with the qualifying phrase "with malice."[14] Here only the state of mind, and not the legality of the killing, is taken into consideration. Occasionally in the Bible hate is identified as a motivating factor for killing. Under this definition some texts may qualify for translation by the English word "murder." But none of those texts also uses the word *rtsh* for the act of killing. The *Oxford English Dictionary* observes that, in Old English, murder was defined as "secret murder." When murder was openly done it was not considered a crime because it was not a matter for the courts. The family of the victim would take care of it.[15] Hence murder was a legal term even in its early usage. This may parallel the notion found in Numbers 35, where it is legal for the גואל (*goʾel*),[16] the "family avenger" to kill a רוצח (*rotseah*), "killer," if the killer is found outside the boundaries of the city of refuge. The family avenger is not guilty of murder when he kills the killer. In traditional societies including ancient Israel many civil and even criminal offenses were settled within or between families. Courts entered into disputes when the families could not come to an agreement and things got out of hand, affecting the broader community, or the dispute was covered under established rules of law. In the article on *rtsh* that appears in the *Theological Dictionary of the Old Testament*, the author, Frank Lothar Hossfeld, comments that it is unlikely that *rtsh* was a legal term because it has no cognate in the legal codes of the ancient Near East.[17] A cognate is a similar word in a related

---

[12] *Oxford English Dictionary*, 13:427

[13] Ludwig Koehler and Walter Baumgartner *The Hebrew and Aramaic Lexicon of the Old Testament* (Leiden: Brill, 1996) 3:1283; Francis Brown, et al., *A Hebrew and English Lexicon of the Old Testament* (Oxford: Clarendon Press, 1906, 1951) 953–54.

[14] Abraham Even-Shoshan, *A New Concordance of the Old Testament* (Jerusalem: Kiryat Sefer, 1989) 1091.

[15] *Oxford English Dictionary*, 10:107.

[16] The גואל (*goʾel*) is a family functionary who has the responsibility to redeem family members or property that is lost to the family and carry out revenge when warranted.

[17] Frank-Lothar Hossfeld, רצח, *Theological Dictionary of the Old Testament*, ed. G. Johannes Botterweck and Helmer Ringgren (Grand Rapids: Eerdmans, 2004) 13:631.

language. This is further evidence that *rtsh* is not a parallel to the English word "murder," because "murder" is a legal term. For the purposes of this book murder is defined as unsanctioned intentional killing of a human being by another human being. Admittedly, intentionality is difficult to perceive in many biblical texts. The phrases "by mistake" and "without knowing," which do appear in the biblical text convey an absence of intentionality. Murder, by this definition, does not include sanctioned (legal) killing as in capital punishment, war, or self-defense.

Frequency of Use of the Word "*rtsh*," "kill," in the Bible

The Hebrew word in question, *rtsh*, appears only thirteen times in its verbal form, thirty-two times in its noun[18] form, typically as a masculine participle functioning as a noun, *rotseah*, "killer," once as "killings," once in the feminine form as "killed," and twice as an adjective.[19] Nahum Sarna writes in his Exodus commentary: "As noted by Rashbam and Bekhor Shor, [*rtsh*] applies only to illegal killing and, unlike other verbs for the taking of life, is never used in the administration of justice. . . ."[20] Rashbam and Bekhor Shor were twelfth-century French rabbis. They were not correct, as the analysis below will demonstrate.

A Study of the Word *rtsh*, "kill"

The following texts indicate that the Hebrew word *rtsh* in its biblical usage extended beyond the idea of "murder," which in English and American law, as well as in colloquial use, is not an adequate translation of the Hebrew word used in Exod 20:13. That verse is best read as "You shall not kill."

All translations in this book are mine unless otherwise indicated.[21] Because translators do not limit the meaning of *rotseah* to "murderer," it

---

[18] Even-Shoshan, *Concordance*, 1091, 1069.

[19] The more frequently used word הרג (*hrg*), "kill," appears 167 times.

[20] Nahum Sarna, *The JPS Torah Commentary: Exodus* (Philadelphia: Jewish Publication Society, 1991) 113.

[21] They are "overly wooden" in order to allow non-readers of biblical Hebrew to see the nuances and ambiguities and judge for themselves. Words that appear in brackets do not appear in the text. They substitute for "he," "him," and "his" in order to create an inclusive-language translation.

will not be the focus of attention, though of necessity there will be some discussion of texts in which this form of the word appears, because interpreters will often point to non-verbal forms of the word (as well as unrelated words) to support their argument that *rtsh* ought to be translated as "murder."

Semantic Range of the Word "kill"

When *rtsh* appears in a list, it is impossible to determine its precise meaning. In the Bible the word *rtsh* appears four times in lists in which the behavior indicated by the use of the verb is prohibited. (It never appears in a list in which the behavior is approved or encouraged.) Although the reader knows that something is not to be done, the nature of what is not to be done is ambiguous. For example, the Ten Commandments appear twice in the Bible in the form of lists (with this commandment at Exod 20:13 and Deut 5:17). There are slight variations in the statement of some of the commandments, but the wording of the sixth commandment is consistent in both places. It reads "You shall not *rtsh*." What kind of killing is being prohibited? Murder? Suicide? War? Capital punishment? Police action? Human sacrifice? Euthanasia? The reader knows that the action is prohibited, but cannot determine the scope of the word *rtsh*. In two other places the word *rtsh* also appears in lists. Both are in books of prophecy. In Jeremiah, on the cusp of the Babylonian invasion, the prophet is warning the people of Judah to not trust the false words of prophets who offer assurances of security. The people cannot continue to violate God's commands and expect to escape disaster. Jeremiah 7:9-10a reads: "Will you steal, *rtsh*, commit adultery, swear to a lie, offer incense to Baal, and go after other gods whom you have not known, and [then] come and stand before me in this house that is called by my name and say 'we are safe'?" It is a rhetorical question. The expected answer is "Of course not!" At an earlier point in time Hosea, a prophet preaching in the northern Israelite kingdom, is accusing the people of lacking truthfulness, faithfulness, and kindness. The word in question appears in the context of a lawsuit. God in the role of prosecutor accuses the people specifically of "swearing, *rtsh*, deceiving, stealing, committing adultery . . ." (Hos 4:2a). Four times the word *rtsh* in its verbal form appears in a list, and its meaning in the list is ambiguous. Those four times are out of a total of only thirteen appearances in the entire Hebrew Bible.

Lists can help us in a limited way with the scope of the meaning of the word in its ancient context. We can ask, "To whom is the list addressed?" "Can the other items on the list help us to understand the targeted one?" In Exod 20:13 the stated audience is the people (העם, *ha'am),* specifically the people whom God brought out of Egyptian slavery, a group identified as "mixed" earlier in Exodus (12:38). "Mixed" probably indicates a heterogeneous group of people, many of whom did not trace their biological roots to the eponymous ancestors[22] of the Israelite tribes (the sons of Jacob and his four wives). The Ten Commandment list in Deuteronomy 5, however, identifies the crowd specifically as "Israel" (5:1), again making reference to slavery in Egypt. The books of Exodus and Deuteronomy emerge out of different sources, and they tell the story of the Exodus in different ways, using different language based upon the audience to whom the books were originally addressed and the scribes who wrote or copied texts (involving their place in history, social and religious issues, use of language, etc.). The list in the Jeremiah text mentioned above is directed only to the people of the southern Israelite kingdom of Judah. By the time of the prophet Jeremiah the northern kingdom of Israel no longer existed, having been conquered by Assyria. Hosea 4:2 also uses the word *rtsh* in a list addressed to the "children of Israel." How does this inform the meaning of the word *rtsh?* It raises the question of limitations. Does it apply only to killing within Israel, or does it include killing of non-Israelites? Hossfeld assumes that the intent is to limit the prohibition to Israelites functioning within the Israelite community,[23] but that may not be the case.

Exodus 20 contains a list of five prohibitions, not just one. None of the ethical injunctions of the Ten Commandments is modified by the language of ethnicity. The commandment does not read "You shall not kill your kin" or "You shall not kill your neighbor." And are we prepared to argue that prohibitions against killing, stealing, lying, coveting, adultery are only limited to behavior within the community of Israel? The story of David's adultery with Bathsheba, the wife of a Hittite, would suggest that in some circles in ancient Israel the ethical directives of Israelite law were extended to the behavior of Israelites in relation to foreigners. The prophet condemns David's behavior and punishes him severely. Adultery is not only an offense against the outsider; it harms the family of the

---

[22] These are the ancestors whose names become those of the tribes. Benjamin is the eponymous ancestor of the Benjaminites.

[23] Hossfeld, רצח, *TDOT* 13:633.

adulterer and the community in which it takes place. Killing also affects not only the family and community of the victim, but the family and community of the killer. People who kill are likely to create enemies who desire to kill them in return, as the Abraham and the Shechemites story in Genesis 34 illustrates. Moreover, killing affects the mental health of the killer and therefore the placidity of the community from which the killer emerged and reshapes the killing ethic itself. This is why the ethical injunctions found in the Ten Commandments are also present in nearly every other society on earth. Another example of an Israelite tradition that extends beyond its own ethnic group is found in Num 15:15-16, which states that there will be one torah (law or instruction) for the Israelite and the foreigner.[24]

Scholars have three other sources to turn to in order to determine the meaning of an ambiguous word: texts in which the meaning of the word is clear from its context, cognate words (words that are similar in related languages), and ancient commentaries (if they exist).

Arabic supplies the only cognate known thus far for the Hebrew word *rtsḥ*. In Arabic a similar word means "break, bruise, crush."[25] The Arabic word does not assist us in our quest to find the more accurate translation.

One must also keep in mind that the meanings of words change over time. The Bible was not composed and written all at once, but over centuries. Moreover, the same word may have different meanings in different communities of the same time period. For example, the word "peculiar" means "distinct" in British English and "weird" in American English. The discussion below demonstrates, however, that the word in question, *rtsḥ*, has different meanings even within the same texts, indicating that in the mind of the writer it had a broader semantic range.

Killing and the Cities of Refuge

According to the Bible, the ancient Israelites were told by God through Moses to set aside cities to which killers could flee if they had not intentionally harmed their victims. In these cities killers were protected from

---

[24] In some ancient Israelite sources outsiders are condemned for ethical violations against other outsiders (e.g., Amos 1–2), which suggests that those sources understood the ethical directives of ancient Israel to extend beyond its borders.

[25] *Rtsḥ*, in Francis Brown, Samuel R. Driver, and Charles A. Briggs, *A Hebrew and English Lexicon of the Old Testament,* tr. Edward Robinson (Oxford: Clarendon Press, 1951) 953.

family members of the victim who would have tried to kill them. This was not just a matter of angry relatives overwrought with grief and anger seeking revenge. In ancient times many matters of justice were worked out within or between families. Certain members of the family were designated to see that justice was done on behalf of the family. In ancient Israel such a person was called a *go'el*. It was acceptable for a family to order the execution of a person who was responsible for the death of one of their family members.[26] This was true whether the death was an accident or intentional. Knowing this, a person who killed another could flee to a city that was designated "a city of refuge."[27] In the city of refuge he or she would be protected for a period of time from the *go'el*[28] of the victim's family. The function of the cities of refuge was to allow for a cooling-off period and an impartial judgment as to whether or not the alleged killer had committed a crime. If it was determined that the person had intentionally and illegally killed the other, protection was no longer granted. Cities throughout Israel were designated cities of refuge so that there would be one in every region proximate to every person who might need a place of safety.

Proposed guidelines for the use and function of the cities of refuge are found in the books of Numbers (ch. 35), Deuteronomy (chs. 4 and 19), and Joshua (chs. 20 and 21). In Numbers the cities of refuge are set aside for those who kill "by mistake." Killers may not be executed until they have had their day in court. The cities protect both Israelites and foreigners. In Deuteronomy, on the other hand, in a different phrase, the cities of refuge are designed for those who kill not "by mistake" as in Numbers, but "without knowing." The texts specify that the killer must not have hated the deceased person in the past (no malice aforethought). The person who was killed is described as a friend (or neighbor) of the killer not an enemy. The word *rtsḥ* appears in these texts, most often in the noun form "killer." In fact, there is only one place in the entire Bible where the noun form appears together with the verbal form of this word in the same sentence, Deut 4:41-42. It reads: "Then Moses set apart three cities when crossing the Jordan eastward, for fleeing there, for a 'killer'

---

[26] "Eye for an eye" justice was not the only way to deal with such offenses.

[27] The cities of refuge existed only on the conceptual level; no textual or archaeological evidence suggests otherwise.

[28] The descriptions of the cities of refuge appear in legal texts or texts that indicate the intended distribution of such cities throughout Israel.

(*rotseah*) that 'kills' (*rtsh*) a friend without knowing and [the killer][29] had not been a hater of [the deceased] in the past." It would be inappropriate to substitute the words murderer and murder in this text because it is clear that the killing was unintentional and hate was not a motive. In the book of Joshua (chs. 20–21), the third text describing the cities of refuge, the action of the killer is not described as "killing," but as "striking dead." The Hebrew word used is not *rtsh*, but *nkh*. There is still the proviso, however, that the death be unintentional. In Joshua the killer is not automatically granted protection in the city of refuge. Rather, the killer must present his or her case before the elders of the city. If the elders believe there is merit in the case as presented by the killer, entrance into the city may be granted. At that point the killer may not be turned over to the *goʾel* (family avenger) who shows up at the gate of the city. But that is not the end of it. A full trial will be held. The killer remains in the city of refuge until the death of the high priest. Though the protocols of the cities of refuge are a little different in Numbers, Deuteronomy, and Joshua, in each case they protect only killers who were not murderers.

In the cities-of-refuge texts the noun *rotseah*, "killer," is used many times to describe a hypothetical person who kills accidentally. The verbal form of the word "kill" appears only three times, once to describe the deed of a person who killed without intent and without hate (Deut 4:42), once to describe the action of the family avenger who kills the killer outside the city of refuge (Num 35:27), and once to describe the penalty meted out to the killer: "someone will kill the killer . . ." (Num 35:30). Nowhere in the cities-of-refuge texts is the action of the killer best described by the English word "murder."

In addition to the references to the cities of refuge, Numbers 35 describes unacceptable types of killing. In those verses the killer is not said to "kill" victims, but to "strike" them with an outcome of death. "Kill" as a verb, the word used in Exod 20:13, is *not* found here to describe the action taken by a murderer, though the noun/participle, *rotseah* (which can be translated "killer" or "murderer"), is found fully eighteen times. It is used to describe a person who uses an iron, wood, or stone tool as a weapon to strike the victim. The person doing the striking is called a *rotseah*. In these cases "murderer" is the best translation.

Another way of identifying a murderer according to this chapter is by the presence of hate or hostility when a person causes the death of another

---

[29] Words that appear in brackets do not actually appear in the text; they substitute for "he," "him," or other gender-exclusive words.

by pushing, throwing a person down, or striking with the hand. The physical action and the emotional state of the killer together determine whether the action was murder. But the word *rtsḥ* is not used to describe the action.

Numbers 35 distinguishes between a murder and an unintentional killing. If there is no hate motive when a person pushes another or throws something against a person and there is no pursuit or a person unintentionally injures another person with a stone, causing a death, a judge will decide what to do. The council will protect the killer from the family avenger.

In Numbers 35 the same word, *rotseaḥ,* is used to describe both a person who intentionally kills another and one who does so unintentionally. This word clearly has a broader semantic range than "murderer," as most scholars admit. Moreover, this chapter permits a type of intentional killing that is legal, as described in the next paragraph.

Killing in the Court of Law

There is one place in Numbers 35 where killing is permissible in the administration of justice. It is given as a general directive to be followed. In Num 35:29-30 the key in the injunction is the presence or absence of witnesses. If a person kills and there are multiple witnesses, the court[30] can order the execution of the person who caused the death. A sentence of death, however, is not permitted on the testimony of only one witness. The deed of the person who kills in this text is described by the word "strike," *nkh.* The action of the court is *rtsḥ,* kill, the same word used in Exod 20:13. The next verse (Num 35:31) indicates that a ransom may not be accepted in exchange for the life of the killer. The killer must die. The verse is not clear about who (if anyone) is to carry out the punishment. The word *rtsḥ* cannot mean murder according to the definition present in the *Oxford English Dictionary* when the court is doing it or allowing it, because it is in the realm of what is legal.

Can an Animal Be Tried for Murder?

The book of Proverbs is filled with advice for daily life. There are many warnings against idleness. In one verse a person who is too lazy to

[30] The word "court" does not appear in this verse. It is assumed that "court" best describes the legal entity presumed.

go out to work or school presents the excuse that a lion may be waiting outside to consume him or her. Proverbs 22:13 reads: "An idle person says, 'a lion is outside! I will be killed (rtsh) in the middle of the street.'" The word rtsh appears in this verse in verbal form, but it cannot mean murder. Animals may indeed kill, but they do not make moral judgments.

Elisha Thinks the King Wants to Murder Him!

There are several places in the Bible where a form of the word rtsh is used but the meaning is unclear. For example, 2 Kings 6 reports that during a severe famine Elisha the prophet is sitting in his house. The king of Israel is distraught when he learns that some people are turning to cannibalism in order to survive. The king sends a messenger to Elisha to get theological counsel. Elisha misinterprets the presence of the messenger and asks "Do you see that the son of this killer (or murderer) has been sent to remove my head . . .?" (6:32). It is unclear why Elisha uses this terminology. Is he calling the unnamed king a murderer? Is he calling the father of the king a murderer? If so, why? Is this an idiom? Elisha thinks the king wants to kill him (literally "to remove his head"), but that is not the case. The messenger comes on behalf of the king to seek counsel on a theological question: "This is the evil from the Lord. Why should I continue to wait for the Lord?" (2 Kings 6:33). The form of the word "kill" that is used in this verse is a participle functioning as a noun. It is likely that the intended meaning is "murderer." The verbal form of the word, however, does not appear.

Did Ahab Murder Naboth?

In 1 Kings 21 the word rtsh appears in its verbal form, but its meaning is still unclear. Ahab is the king in Israel. Jezebel is his queen. Jezebel is also the daughter of a Sidonian (non-Israelite) king. Having grown up in a royal household, she is accustomed to a particular form of monarchy that allows the king to do as he pleases. According to 1 Kings 21, Ahab wants to purchase a parcel of land from Naboth, a commoner, to turn it into a vegetable garden, because the land is near the palace. He makes the request of Naboth and offers him either a better vineyard or silver for it. Naboth refuses. When Ahab tells Jezebel what happened, she responds that he should not worry about it because she will give the vineyard to Ahab. Jezebel writes letters slandering Naboth and arranges for his death. After Naboth is dead, Jezebel informs Ahab and tells him to possess the land. He does. At this point Elijah, the prophet of God, confronts Ahab. Using the language of the prophetic formula, "Thus says Yhwh," he asks: "Have you killed *(rtsḥ)* and also possessed . . .?" This is unexpected. Yes, Ahab has possessed the land, but he did not kill anyone. According to the story, Jezebel arranged for the death of Naboth and Ahab did not learn about it until after the deed was done. He neither killed Naboth nor consented to his death nor arranged for it. At best Ahab is, in modern terminology, an accessory after the fact. He is not a murderer. Yet he is accused of having killed Naboth. Is it possible that in a longer form of this story Ahab did play a role in the death that is not represented here? Perhaps, but in the narrative as it appears in the Bible as we have it, Ahab did not murder anyone. Elijah condemned both Ahab and Jezebel. The meaning of *rtsḥ*, "kill," in this text is unclear. But it does appear as a verb.

Is Murder the Only Type of Unacceptable Killing?

Murder is not the only form of unacceptable killing. Using a common literary technique, Isa 1:21 contrasts past and present in the village of Neemanah. The village used to be full of justice and righteousness. Now it is full of *rtsḥ*, killing. It is clear from the context of the sentence that *rtsḥ* is something undesirable. A list of terrible things that are being done in the city is provided. They include theft and bribery. The word here can refer to murder, but also to other types of killing of human beings: suicides, preventable accidents, capital punishment, and mistreatment of the poor that leads to their deaths. The word appears here as a participle and is therefore excluded from our list of verbal usages of the word *rtsḥ*.

Rtsḥ appears in its verbal form in Ps 62:4 (English 62:3), but its meaning is unclear. The translators of the English versions have adopted a variety of English words to translate *rtsḥ* in this text: *NRSV* "batter," *JPS* "crush," *NIV* "throw down," *NKJV* "slain," as an act of justice, and *NAB* "beating them down." *NRSV*, *JPS*, and *NIV* use "murder" in Exod 20:13, but not here. My translation is, "How long will you attack a person? You kill, all of you, like a leaning wall, like a pushed-in wall." The verse appears to imply that people are not directly killing others. They set up situations, though, that eventually cause the death of others, psychologically, socially, spiritually, but probably not physically. The word appears here as a verb, but its meaning is unclear because the meaning of other phrases in the verse is unclear.

In the preceding texts, four out of thirteen times, the verb *rtsh* appears on a list; four times it is clear from the context that murder cannot be the intended meaning because the killings are unintentional, carried out by an animal or persons having the authority to do so. Twice the meaning of the word is unclear from the context, either because the context is unintelligible or because there is nothing in the narrative to suggest that the person actually killed anyone or participated in the planning of the death of the person.

Yes, *rtsh* Does Mean Murder—Sometimes

Rtsh does have the sense of murder in some verses in the Bible, though even in some of these the intended meaning may be a different sort of killing than the kind that would get one convicted in a modern court of law. The following narrative, though it does not actually contain the word "kill" in its verbal form, is instructive. At the end of Judges (chs. 19–20), a horrific story is narrated: a woman is turned over to a mob that abuses her all night. The woman is found the next morning on the threshold of the house where her husband is staying. When the husband addresses her, she does not speak. He then takes her home and cuts her body up into pieces and sends them throughout the tribes of Israel. Scholars think this action represented a kind of war cry and threat. (A similar story is told in 1 Samuel 11 involving oxen rather than a human being. A ritual cutting-up of animals is described in Genesis 15.) The message was that if a tribe did not send warriors to right the wrong, that tribe would be cut up just like the woman. The woman is referred to in Judg 20:4 as a "killed" or "murdered" woman, using a participial form of the same word *rtsh*, that is used in Exod 20:13. The question is: who killed her, and is this rightly to be understood as murder? The story never says that the mob killed her. It reads in part: "They knew her and they abused her all night . . ." (Judg 19:25). The husband may have killed her when he cut her up. If he did, then it would appear that he murdered her. Yet he is never accused of murder by the narrator or any other character in the story. The husband has been offended, and all the tribes of Israel come out to support him, but what was the crime, if there was one? The murder of his wife/concubine? The abuse of the wife/concubine? Property damage? This is a very strange story, and it is an example of "everyone doing as he or she pleased" (Judg 21:25), not an example of appropriate behavior. The reason why, for our purposes, it is important to determine who killed the woman is that if the mob killed her this is an example of murder. But why does the text not say that the mob killed her? If the husband killed her, it may also be murder, but he would hardly have the support of all the tribes of Israel if he murdered her, unless he killed her but did not murder her. How would that be possible? It would be possible if the killing was a ritualistic killing or a mercy killing. The latter is unlikely, since the man shows no compassion for the woman. A pagan ritualistic killing that would have been acceptable seems possible.[31] If a ritual killing is intended, then "kill" is the better translation. *Rtsh* appears here in the form of a feminine participle,[32] and it functions as a descriptive adjective. This is the only place in the Bible where the feminine participial form of our word is found. This feminine participle ought to be classed with the masculine participles rather than the verbal forms. The participle form is granted a broader meaning. Although the verbal form of *rtsh* does not appear here, this text is often cited as one where the root meaning is murder.

Readers of English translations of the Bible cannot always tell whether one Hebrew word is being used consistently or a variety of Hebrew words are being used and translated into the same English word. In Job 24:14 and Ps 94:6 the killing of the poor and the needy are listed among crimes

---

[31] Roberto Green thinks that the statement "everyone was doing as he or she pleases" is a reference to traditional Canaanite practices that were adopted by Israelites. Roberto R. W. Green, *The Role of Human Sacrifice in the Ancient Near East* (Missoula: Scholars, 1975) 151. Green notes that graves containing humans that have been cut in half or have body parts missing, with indications that they were cut off, have been found at Gezer (p. 153). He does not discuss the possibility of human sacrifice as a battle cry. William Beers suggests that sacrifice is a way to permit men to kill legally, to bond with each other, and to create a separation between themselves and the victim. In Judges the killing appears to be acceptable since neither a character in the story nor the narrator suggests it was illegal. The abuse of the woman was unacceptable not because it hurt the woman, but because it destroyed property owned by a man. The men bond as they go off to war against the tribe of Benjamin. The woman is the other from whom the man and the men separate themselves. See William Beers, *Women and Sacrifice* (Detroit: Wayne State University Press, 1992) 144–45.

[32] Even-Shoshan places the masculine participle form in a separate place in the concordance and gives it a separate definition. The feminine pariticple, however, is placed with the verbal root.

being committed in the community. Job 24:14 reads: "A killer arises when it is light[33] and kills the poor and the needy." The person in this verse is a killer or murderer, but the crime is not called *rtsh*. Another Hebrew word, *qtl*[34] *(qatal)*, which also means kill, is used. The meaning of "kill" in this text hints at intentionality and brazenness, and yet it is done in broad daylight! The first half of ch. 24 contains a long list of ways in which widows and orphans are being abused. They include depriving widows and orphans of their livelihood and the fruit of their labor and misuse of the law to favor the privileged. All of these are recognizable as ways that the poor, widows, and orphans are typically treated in too many societies. The meaning of the word "kill" in this context is "brutally mistreat." The harsher word "kill" is used to create revulsion in the reader toward the deed and the ones doing it. But it is unlikely that the word is referring to murdering the widows and orphans in the common way in which that word is used in English. It is unlikely that the writer means that the privileged are literally shooting arrows at the widows and orphans or crushing their heads with stones.[35] If such deeds as listed in Job 24 were done today, the persons doing them would not be charged with murder in an American court, though they might be found guilty of a host of other crimes.

In two texts *rtsh* is used similarly to *qtl* in the text just mentioned. Psalm 94 is calling for vengeance upon the wicked who mistreat the most vulnerable members of society. A list of atrocities follows. In the sixth verse of the psalm, two parallel phrases are placed in tandem. The first reads: "Widow and foreigner they kill," the second: "orphans they kill." The second phrase contains the same word used in Exod 20:13, *rtsh*. The first uses another Hebrew word, *hrg* (also "kill"). The *NRSV* translates "They kill the widow and the stranger, they murder the orphan." In

---

[33] The Hebrew says light. The *JPS, NRSV,* and *NIV* understand the reference to be to the evening. See Adele Berlin and Marc Zwi Brettler, eds., *The Jewish Study Bible* (Oxford: Oxford University Press, 2004) 1536 n. b-b. The *NAB* reads "When there is no light the murderer rises. . . ." It is likely, given the list of charges that surrounds the text, that the verse is referring to abuses that occur in broad daylight as well as those that occur under the cover of darkness.

[34] Koehler-Baumgartner (3:1092) indicates that this is an Akkadian loan word used in the sense of "to kill a sacrificial animal" or a "symbolic act accompanying a treaty ceremony."

[35] According to Hossfeld, Frank Crüsemann agrees with this understanding: רצח, *TDOT* 13:633, citing Frank Crüsemann, *Bewahrung der Freiheit: das Thema des Dekalogs in sozialgeschichtlicher Perspektive* (Munich: Kaiser, 1983) 28–29.

this bicolon[36] the "kill" words likely mean "brutally mistreat to the point of shortening a natural lifespan."[37]

The prophet Hosea scolds Israel and Judah and pleads with them to return to God. Examples of the people's evil deeds are listed. They include planned killing (6:9). "They kill on the way to Shechem because they made a plan."[38] This is a text in which the phrase that includes the word *rtsh* probably means murder. But we only know that because the word itself is modified by the phrase "with a plan."[39] It is murder because the context is crime and because the killing is done with a plan. This is an intentional illegal killing, "murder," but the word alone is not able to convey that meaning.

Another occurrence of the verb *rtsh* appears in a simile in Deut 22:26, where murder is compared to a woman who is raped in the countryside. The context is a series of directions as to how to determine whether or not rape or consensual sexual activity has taken place. If there is sexual activity between a man and a woman in the countryside and the woman claims that she was raped, the woman is to be believed and the man shall die. "You shall not do anything to the young woman. She has committed no sin worthy of death. This is like when a man rises up against his neighbor and kills him." The latter statement is a simile. Murder and rape, two crimes that can be committed without witnesses, are compared. The word "rises up" is the same word used of Cain in Gen 4:8b. "Cain rose up against his brother, Abel, and killed him." The word *rtsh* does not appear in this text. It is also unclear as to whether Cain intended to kill Abel. However, murder is likely the intended meaning in Deut 22:26. The verbal form of the word does appear there.

Murder is perhaps the best translation of רצח, *rtsh*, in three verses. *Rtsh* appears in a verbal form as "murder" outside of the participle three times, once in Ps 94:6 (maybe), once in Hos 6:9 (within a phrase), and once in Deut 22:26. This means that out of thirteen occurrences of the

---

[36] A bicolon is a poetic structure in which there are two lines that relate to each other in some way.

[37] It has been reported that street children were literally killed, shot, in the streets of Brazil during the late twentieth century as a way of getting rid of them. Could similar direct killing of orphans have occurred in ancient times? The widows, orphans, and strangers who suffered such abuse were without adult male protectors.

[38] *NRSV, NAB,* and *NIV* have "crime." *JPS* has "depravity."

[39] Most of the English Bible versions do not translate the Hebrew word *zimmah* as "plan." *NRSV* translates "monstrous crime," *JPS* "depravity," *NIV* "shameful crimes," *NAB* "monstrous crime."

finite verb in the Hebrew Bible, רצח can be demonstrated probably to mean murder at most only three times.

Summary

The definition of רוצח *(rotseaḥ)* as a noun/participle has always allowed for a variety of translations. No one has disputed that. However, the word רצח *(rtsḥ)*, the verbal form of the same word, is being translated "murder," as is evident from a perusal of the late-twentieth-century Bible translations, nearly every time it appears in the Bible. A summary of the usages of the word רצח *(rtsḥ)* follows:

Ambiguous: four occurrences: appears in lists (Exod 20:13; Deut 5:17; Jer 7:9; Hos 4:2)

Action of an animal: one occurrence: Prov 22:13

Court action: one occurrence: Num 35:29-30

Legal action by a גואל *(goʾel):* one occurrence: Num 35:26-28

Unintentional killing: one occurrence: Deut 4:41-42

Charge made against a person who did not plan or commit a killing but benefited afterward: one occurrence: 1 Kings 21:19

Unclear: one occurrence: Ps 62:4

Murder: three occurrences: Hos 6:9 (as part of a phrase), Ps 94:6 (perhaps), Deut 22:26

Out of the thirteen times that the verb רצח *(rtsḥ)* appears in the Hebrew Bible (except for participles), four times the texts clearly indicate that murder is not the appropriate translation of רצח *(rtsḥ)* because other meanings are clearly stated. Four times the meaning is ambiguous because it appears in a list. Clearly something is being prohibited, but is the prohibition limited to murder as opposed to other forms of killing (war, police actions, suicide, capital punishment, human sacrifice, etc.)? Once the meaning is unclear. Once it is used to describe the action of a person who did not plan or commit a murder (metaphor, accessory after the fact, benefiting from a crime, hyperbole). Perhaps three times "murder" is the best translation. Because the semantic range of the word is broader than the English word murder, the weight of the evidence is clearly against automatically translating רצח (*rtsḥ*) as murder in ambiguous verses in lists such as Exod 20:13 and Deut 5:17.

If *rtsḥ* Clearly Does Not Mean "murder" Everywhere It Is Found in the Bible, Why Do Translators Insist That It Does?

Bible translators do not come to their task uninfluenced by their faith traditions or lack thereof, political commitments, historical, social, and cultural locations. Most people either support killing traditions such as war and capital punishment or are resigned to them. A "you shall not murder" translation fits their theological or political commitments better than a "you shall not kill" translation.

Typically a "murder" translation is supported by an appeal to other Scripture texts in which God supposedly commands killing. Exodus 21 with its list of offenses that merit capital punishment is nearly always cited, followed by war texts in Joshua, Samuel, and Kings. If God commands Israelites to kill in some texts, they say, there cannot be a general prohibition against killing in another text that is represented as coming from the same God. *Rtsḥ*, therefore, must mean "murder," and not "kill" in general. The theological assumption is that God must hold to a consistent ethic. But these Scripture-interprets-Scripture arguments are not as straightforward as they seem.

There Are Pro-Killing Traditions and Anti-Killing Traditions in the Bible

First, we cannot assume that because texts appear in a particular place or order in the Bible, that was their original setting. The order in which the books were placed varied over time and place. This is true in both the Jewish and Christian traditions. Within some of the biblical books, the hand of editors who moved material around and shaped it is in evidence. One can see this by comparing the Septuagint (an early Greek translation) with the Hebrew Bible, or by comparing the same text in various Dead Sea Scroll manuscripts, or by a careful literary study of the text. The book of Psalms, for example, has certain types of psalms gathered together in one place. Praise psalms were collected at the end of the book. In the book of Proverbs, sayings with "three and four" structures are gathered together in the second half of ch. 30. This does not mean that they were all written at the same time and place. It simply means that similar material was gathered together in one place.

Although Exodus 21 with its list of "capital" offenses appears right after Exodus 20, the source of each may have been entirely different. Exodus 21 may have been written without awareness of Exodus 20 or vice versa. Exodus 21 differs from Exodus 20 in a number of ways. Exodus 21 is casuistic or case law, whereas Exodus 20 is apodictic law. Casuistic law has the structure, "If a person does such and such, such and such will be the result." Exodus 21:17 exhibits the structure of casuistic law: "Whoever curses father or mother will surely die." Apodictic law, on the other hand, is structured as a straightforward statement, usually in the negative: "You shall not kill." Moreover, the vocabulary in use in Exodus 21 is different from that of Exodus 20. When someone kills someone in Exodus 21, most often the deed is expressed using a form of the word *nkh*, which means "strike." A qualifying phrase may specify that the victim dies. A sample verse reads: "One who strikes a person and death ensues, will die" (Exod 21:12). If *rtsh* was known to be the appropriate term for murder, it would surely have been used in Exod 21:12, but it is not. Either the authors of Exodus 21 did not have that word in their vocabulary, or they did not deem it an appropriate word for the deed. The word *rtsh*, in fact, never appears in Exodus 21. Moreover, the phrase "will die" or "will surely die" without a specification as to who will cause the death is translated in modern versions more aggressively. They become "shall be put to death" *(TANAKH, NRSV, NAB)*, and "must be put to death" *(NIV)*, which suggests that the community is to act against that person. But that is not the only way to interpret the phrase. The traditional Jewish interpretation of this verse, given the grammatical and syntactical structure that is employed, is that God, not the human community, will bring about the death. In this reading the text does not support capital punishment, because the human community is not expected to take action.

Supporting W. Günther Plaut in the line of argument that the Bible permits killing in some texts is Moshe Weinfeld, who points out several other places in the Torah where there is straightforward prohibition against "murder," to use his terminology. They are Exod 21:12, Lev 24:21, Num 35:30, and Deut 19:11-13; 27:16.[40] However, in none of these cases is

---

[40] Moshe Weinfeld, "The Uniqueness of the Decalogue and Its Place in Jewish Tradition," in Ben-Zion Segal, ed., *The Ten Commandments in History and Tradition,* English

the word *rtsḥ* used. Exodus 21:12 and Lev 24:21 use participial forms of *nkh*, which means to strike. Leviticus 24:21 literally reads: "one who strikes a person will be caused to die." Since the word "strike" in Hebrew does not automatically indicate that a death ensued, this may in fact be envisioning a less-than-lethal encounter. A modifying phrase indicating that the victim dies as a result of being struck is added in some texts. In Num 35:30 the deed is again described as "striking." Permission is granted there for the killing of a killer. The same verbal root is used for the one executing the person who struck another as for the person who did the deed. The executioner is not a murderer, but a representative of the community who is authorized to carry out the killing on behalf of the community. In Deut 19:11-13 the deed is again "strike." "He struck a person and he died. . . ." In each case the prohibition or punishment is against a deed described using a form of the word "strike," and not the word used in Exod 20:13.

"Aha!" you are saying now. So in Lev 24:21 and Num 35:30 God permits or requires the execution of persons! This supports the thesis that *rtsḥ* could be read as "murder" and not "kill," because certain types of killing are permitted! Read on.

Some who reject a "kill" translation for Exod 20:13 think that "the Bible" as it exists today was one entity in ancient times. The Bible in the opinion of most modern critical scholars is not a single unified entity, but a collection of diverse materials with diverse theological viewpoints. The ancient Israelites struggled with questions of how to understand God and God's relationship with humankind. Modern scholars generally reject attempts at harmonizing texts in favor of placing them in their own contexts, whether literary, historical, sociological, or theological. Yes, a killing theology emerges in some texts, but those texts need not theologically trump non-killing texts. Even where a penalty of death is stated in the Bible, often the question of who, if anyone, is to carry out the penalty is vague. Many modern commentators place that authority in the hands of the state or the nation even though such entities did not exist in ancient times and would not have been in the mind of the biblical author. Moreover, biblically speaking, if God reserves the right to kill, this does not mean that humans have the same right. The infamous phrase from Gen 9:6, "the one who sheds the blood of a human, by a

edited by Gershon Levi (Jerusalem: Magnes Press, Hebrew Univeristy, 1990) 2, n. 5. Cf. W. Günther Plaut, *The Torah: a modern commentary* (New York: Union of American Hebrew Congregations, 1974).

human his blood will be shed," is nearly always read as a command for capital punishment. More likely this is a reflection on the escalation of violence. The way of bloodshed only leads to more bloodshed. This statement need not be read as a command. No imperative is used.

"Scripture interprets Scripture" proponents also point to the books of Joshua and Judges as proof that killing is permitted in the Hebrew Bible. This is particularly disturbing. Few scholars, rabbis, or pastors point to those books as models of appropriate behavior. Indeed, the critique that appears at the end of Judges: "In those days there was no king in Israel. Everyone did what was right in his [or her] eyes" appears to be an ancient criticism of the violence and mayhem described earlier in that book, and perhaps in the book of Joshua as well.[41]

Further, people tend to assume that, according to the Bible, God commanded a battle or killing when in fact the text never indicates that God had anything to do with the killing. The story of the battle of Jericho is one case in point. Chapter 6 tells what God said, what Joshua said, and what the people did. The last instruction God gives is, "The wall of the city will collapse under itself and the people will go up . . ." (Josh 6:5). Notice that God never told Joshua to kill anyone or to have the Israelites kill anyone. Interpreters of the Bible who support killing or who are resigned to it read the Bible and translate it into more violence than even it contains.

Moreover, within the Bible there are summary statements of ethical principles that in the mind of some biblical traditions are superior to other guidelines. Micah 6:8, "What does YHWH seek from you except to do justice, love kindness, and walk humbly with your God," would be one. "You shall not kill" is another.

The Nature of the Ten Commandments Argues Against a "murder" Translation

A final consideration is the nature of the Ten Commandments. All the other commandments that are stated in the negative prohibit behavior that is widespread: stealing, adultery, coveting, lying. It is also behavior

---

[41] Susan Niditch in her study of the ethics of war in the Hebrew Bible notes that there is an uneasiness within the Bible itself with its war traditions. See Susan Niditch, *War in the Hebrew Bible: A Study in the Ethics of Violence* (Oxford: Oxford University Press, 1993) ch. 7.

that is controllable. Can I get away with cheating on my income tax? Can I enter into this office romance without my spouse finding out? Most adults in the course of their lives will have to make ethical choices that relate to all of these, and it is possible to make an ethical decision to obey or disobey the stipulation. But in spite of what many people may believe if they watch enough television, the crime of murder is relatively rare. Most people are never faced with the question of whether or not to murder a particular person. Indeed, most crimes of murder are crimes of passion or are committed by those who are not constrained by ethical principles. In the Bible few crimes of murder are reported: Joab murders Abner, Cain murders Abel (maybe—if Cain's conscious intent was to extinguish the life of Abel), Jael murders Sisera (unless this is considered an act of war, in which case it is not murder). Saul thinks about murdering David but does not succeed. Humans are fascinated with crimes of murder precisely because they are rare. Most people manage to get through their entire lives without murdering anyone or seriously considering murdering anyone. Killing, however, is more widespread than murdering. Although most people do not directly kill anyone in their entire lives, most adults are complicit in killing as part of a community that executes or participates in war. The community gives its collective assent to capital punishment and war. The commandments as listed in Exodus 20 have more internal consistency if they all apply to behavior that is common and that can be constrained because the persons who read them or hear them can also obey them. It is unlikely that the author intends to prohibit behavior in which people do not typically engage.

This chapter has presented a biblical argument against the automatic assumption that the commandment "You shall not kill" must be understood as "You shall not murder." First, it is clear that the Hebrew word *rtsḥ* does not mean "murder" everywhere it is found in the Bible. Second, it is inappropriate to harmonize Scripture rather than letting the various theological traditions in the Bible speak for themselves. The English word "murder" is a restricted legal term. Last, the Ten Commandments are meant to be general and not to refer to one particular, rarely committed crime.

What else drives the movement toward the more limited interpretation of the sixth commandment? Each of the large biblical traditions has dealt with the commandment in its own way. The next two chapters examine the changed wording in evangelical Protestantism and mainline Protestantism. The fourth and fifth chapters examine the "You shall not kill" commandment in Judaism and Roman Catholicism. Roman Catholicism is the only major tradition that maintains the "kill" reading.

Chapter 2

The Sixth Commandment in Evangelical Protestantism

The term evangelical[1] dates back to the Reformation, but it has meant different things in different places and time periods. In Europe evangelical is sometimes used as a descriptive term for Protestants in general or Protestant denominations that are not the official state church. In the United States at the beginning of the twenty-first century evangelical[2] generally designates movements that emerged in the middle of the twentieth century within denominations (or whole denominations that so self-designate) that emphasize the salvific nature of the Christ event, the importance of being "born again," and the need to proclaim the Good News. In the first half of the twentieth century evangelicalism was largely identified with fundamentalism. That changed after the Second World War. A new evangelical movement that was middle-class, engaged in critical thought, and thoroughly integrated into modern society emerged.

---

[1] The English word evangelical is derived from the Greek word *evangelizō*, meaning preach or proclaim good news. It appears in the New Testament.

[2] For a brief history and description of American evangelicalism and its understanding of the Bible see Stanley J. Grenz, "Nurturing the Soul, Informing the Mind," in Vincent Bacote, Laura C. Miguelez, and Dennis L. Okholm, eds., *Evangelicals & Scripture: Tradition, Authority, and Hermeneutics* (Downers Grove, IL: InterVarsity Press, 2004). Church historians originally referred to this movement as "new evangelicalism" (ibid. 34ff.). Grenz credits Harold Ockenga with coining the phrase.

The characteristic of evangelicals that is significant for this book is their high view of the authority and inspiration of Scripture. That high view leads them to value the words of Scripture (not just the ideas). Fundamentalists and the most theologically conservative evangelicals believe that the Bible is verbally inspired and inerrant (without error at least in the autographs or original documents). Most evangelicals avoid that language and prefer terminology such as infallible[3] or "reliable for faith and practice" because they recognize that there are issues involving translation and the lack of the original manuscripts that make the former terminology difficult to support. In either case the words of Scripture are important. For evangelicals, the Bible is the primary source of authority for Christians. Most would say it is the *only* source of authority *(sola scriptura).* In their view it *is* or *contains* God's word to humankind. With this level of commitment to the words of Scripture, one would expect evangelicals to be particularly suspicious of any changes to the biblical text. And they usually are.

The King James Version Reads "Thou shalt not kill"

The "King James" Bible (the *Authorized Version*) was by far the translation of choice for evangelicals throughout the twentieth century.[4] As new evangelical translations emerged, particularly at the end of the century, evangelicals adopted them. The new translations were not only more understandable because they were written in contemporary English, but they were more attractive visually and available in a wide variety of forms, including electronic. The new translations were also geared to targeted markets such as women (pink covers), the military (*The Soldier's New Testament,* with the insignia of the different branches of the service on the front),[5] and the coveted teen market. An interesting shift occurred. The new translations did not always replace the King James Version. They were used alongside it. Indeed, some evangelicals consider the King James Version to be the ur-text of the Bible. The website of the

---

[3] Infallible means that there are no errors in the theological ideas expressed in the Bible.

[4] In 1999 the *Holman Christian Standard Bible,* promoted among the Southern Baptists, translated "murder," but by then this was becoming a standard practice.

[5] Broadman and Holman Publishing Co. See Bibles at the website, www .broadmanholman.com.

Indianapolis Baptist Temple, a fundamentalist Christian congregation, expresses this idea as follows: "The King James version of Holy Scriptures is the supreme authority of faith and practice. . . . the King James Bible has been preserved by God for English speaking people today. . . . We believe other translations contain the Word of God and may be helpful for personal study but the King James Bible is the Word of God."[6] When confronted with a textual difficulty, evangelicals are frequently heard to say, "I'll check it in the King James" indicating that, for them, that is the source text.

The New International Version Reads
"You shall not murder"

The most popular of the new Bible translations of the late twentieth century, the *New International Version* (*NIV*, 1973), was the work of a committee of evangelical scholars from a variety of denominations. The *NIV* is to some degree a response to the much reviled (by evangelicals) *Revised Standard Version*, which was the work of mainline Protestant scholars. One focus of the ire of the evangelicals was the decision by the *Revised Standard Version* committee to change the translation of the Hebrew word *ʿalmah* in Isa 7:14 from "virgin" to "young woman."[7] For evangelicals this adjustment in the wording seemed to call into question a core doctrine, the virginity of Mary, the mother of Jesus. The *NIV* retained the word "virgin" in Isa 7:14.[8] In light of this history it is most surprising that the translators of the *NIV* could change, without a word of protest from the evangelical community, an equally significant word in the Ten Commandments. "You shall not kill" became "You shall not murder" in Exod 20:13. No explanation for the change was given, and "kill" did not even appear as an alternate translation in a textual note. So

[6] Found under the Position Paper heading at the website of the Indianapolis Baptist Temple, indianapolisbaptisttemple.com/position.php.

[7] See Bruce M. Metzger, "The Revised Standard Version," in Lloyd R. Bailey, ed., *The Word of God: A Guide to English Versions of the Bible* (Atlanta: John Knox, 1982) 33. Daniel B. Wallace, "History of the English Bible, part IV," found on the website of the Biblical Studies Foundation, http://www.bible.org/docs/soapbox/4versions.htm, points to Isa 7:14 and the change in wording from "virgin" to "young woman" as being at the center of the controversy.

[8] For an analysis of the *RSV* controversy see Peter S. Thuessen, "The Great RSV Controversy," in his *In Discordance with the Scriptures: American Protestant Battles over Translating the Bible* (Oxford: Oxford University Press, 1999).

insignificant was this change that neither of two books that trace the history and process of the *NIV* translation, providing examples of changes made, mentions Exod 20:13.[9] Why?

When "You shall not kill" Became "You shall not murder"

By the 1960s the argument that the word "kill" in the Ten Commandments really means "murder" was being used by evangelicals, even though the primary Bible translation used by evangelicals, the King James Version, did not read "murder." In that decade the popular translations of the Bible that read "murder" were the Jewish Publication Society's *Torah* and the *New American Standard Bible*. A smattering of other Christian translations used "murder," though none of these (except the *English Revised* in England, 1885) were widely used. They include *Young's Literal Translation* (1898), *The Complete Bible in Modern English* (1922), *The Bible: An American Translation* (1931), Moffat (1935), and Amplified (1959). The *Scofield Reference Bible*, though not a new translation, was very influential in some evangelical (dispensationalist) circles in the twentieth century. It contained study notes attached to a King James translation. In the 1967 edition of the Scofield Bible a note indicated that "kill" really meant "murder" in the sixth commandment. The earlier Scofield did not have this note. The Scofield Bible notes may have influenced some in the evangelical community to read "murder" where "kill" appeared in the King James Bible. Cyrus H. Gordon, who is identified as a conservative Jew, wrote an article that appeared in the influential evangelical publication *Christianity Today* in the 1960s entitled "The Ten Commandments."[10] Of the sixth commandment he writes that it is "not directed against killing in general. . . . This commandment does not apply . . . to capital punishment . . . nor does it apply to killing the enemy on the battlefield."[11] In 1966 an editorial in the same magazine suggesting that clergy need to speak about the commandment in the context of the war in Vietnam for the benefit of soldiers and prospective

---

[9] See Kenneth L. Barker, ed., *The NIV: The Making of a Contemporary Translation* (Grand Rapids: Zondervan, 1986) and Burton L. Goddard, *The NIV Story* (New York: Vantage Press, 1989).

[10] Cyrus H. Gordon, "The Ten Commandments," *Christianity Today* 8 (April 10, 1964).

[11] Ibid. 627.

soldiers generated letters to the editor stating that the commandment did not apply to war.[12] John I. Durham's careful examination of the word and contemporary scholarship on it for the Word Commentary series concludes that one cannot say with certainty that there was an earlier narrow understanding of the word that related to blood revenge and a later understanding that was broader, as Brevard Childs[13] claims. But what is certain, in his opinion, is that the commandment prohibits killing persons within the covenant community. He writes: "its basic prohibition was against killing, for whatever cause, under whatever circumstances, and by whatever method, a fellow-member of the covenant community."[14] Durham, therefore, retains the "kill" reading and interprets it broadly, but only within the covenant community. Durham does allow for capital punishment, presumably of members of the community, and war. Other factors, theological and existential, were probably as significant in the change of wording.

Mainstreaming of Evangelicals

In the early twentieth century conservative evangelicals and fundamentalists sometimes found themselves in polar opposition to policies and practices of mainstream society and the government on issues such as the teaching of evolution in schools, and alcohol and tobacco use. That wariness toward the government began to change in the latter half of the twentieth century when evangelicals infiltrated the military, public school boards, and the government in order to promote Christian moral values in those institutions. Independent Christian schools sprang up, sometimes in opposition to the desegregation of public schools. Many of these schools inserted a heavy dose of patriotism into the curriculum. The author remembers visiting a school where children sat in booths doing independent work. When a child finished a project he or she would wave an American flag to get the teacher's attention. An April 2004 survey reported by the public television broadcast *Religion and Ethics Newsweekly* showed that Euro-American evangelicals support the mili-

[12] "The Church and the Viet Nam-Bound Soldier", *Christianity Today* 10 (May 13, 1966) 834. The letters appear in *Christianity Today* 10 (July 8, 1966).

[13] Brevard S. Childs, *The Book of Exodus: a critical theological commentary* (Philadelphia: Westminster, 1974) 419–23. See Chapter Four below for more on Childs' interpretation of the sixth commandment.

[14] John I. Durham, *Exodus*. WBC (Waco, TX: Word Books, 1987) 293.

tary to a greater extent than the general public.[15] Most evangelical (and mainline) church hymnals of the twentieth century contain a number of patriotic selections that are sung on the Sundays closest to Memorial Day and the Fourth of July. The most popular of these are "My Country's 'Tis of Thee," "The Star-Spangled Banner," "America the Beautiful," and the "Battle Hymn of the Republic." This seems odd for churches that claim to proclaim a message that is transnational and universal in scope. In the latter half of the twentieth century being patriotic in the United States started to mean being pro-military and pro-war. Individuals and organizations that opposed the Gulf War or the invasion of Iraq, for example, were considered unpatriotic. Churches that are pro-military and pro-war of necessity have to come to terms with killing and the sixth commandment, because killing is inevitable in war.

"You shall not kill" in the
Southern Baptist Convention

The largest of the evangelical traditions, the Southern Baptist Convention, meeting a month after the United States entered the First World War in May of 1917, declared its support of the war effort. But after that a steady stream of peace statements were adopted with some frequency. In 1940 the Convention urged the United States not to become involved in World War II. In that year, before the attack on Pearl Harbor, many Americans were opposed to U.S. involvement in what was seen as a European war. But Southern Baptist sentiments were not entirely based on isolationist ideology. The Convention had been supportive of a conference of nations to promote disarmament in 1921.[16] In 1932 a resolution was adopted by the Convention stating that ". . . we oppose the continued large expenditure by the Government for military and naval equipment . . . we oppose military training in the schools and colleges . . . we favor full and complete disarmament[17]. . . . We reaffirm our hearty approval of the international agreement to abolish war as a national

[15] At www.pbs.org/wnet/religionandethics/week733/results.doc.

[16] "Resolution on Peace," 1921, at sbc.net.

[17] An exception was made for police protection and defense of national borders. These statements are under the title "Social Service Committee Recommendation (adopted)," May 1932, under "Resolutions" at sbc.net. It is found under the word search "disarmament," but not under the year. Copyright © 1999–2005 Southern Baptist Convention.

policy."[18] The statement cites the "incompatibility of war with the ethical principles of our Lord Jesus Christ."[19] A resolution passed at the 1940 Convention continued in the same vein, stating that "because war is contrary to the mind and spirit of Christ, we believe that no war should be identified with the will of Christ. Our churches should not be made agents of war propaganda or recruiting stations. War thrives on and is perpetuated by hysteria, falsehood, and hate. . . ."[20] In the middle of the Second World War the Southern Baptists recognized that Baptists were serving in the armed forces, though they did not explicitly express support of the war. They called upon their own Education Commission to assemble "facts and principles" that would be sent to Baptist senators to begin to work on a peace plan to be implemented when the war was over.[21] In 1948 a further resolution noted that peace does not emerge out of war:

> We recognize the necessity of strong national defense, but we repudiate the idea that world peace can be established by military might. Behind our military defense, and more powerful is the Spirit of Peace. The diplomacy of demand must be accompanied by the diplomacy of friendliness and just and aggressive proposals for the well-being of all nations. We urge against all military policies that would, by becoming fixed patterns in our national structure, militarize the thinking and outlook of our people. We urge that in the diplomatic procedure of our government the voices, not only of military men, but of the scientists, educators, economists and spiritual leaders of the nation be heard. We further urge that the Christians of America commit themselves and their citizenship to the Prince of Peace who would substitute love for hate and neighborliness for war.[22]

The statement also rejected the fatalism in the mindset that "war is inevitable."[23] The Southern Baptists were never entirely pacifist in their theology. They always supported defense of the home territory on its

---

[18] "Social Service Committee Recommendation (adopted)," May 1932, at sbc.net. Copyright © 1999–2005 Southern Baptist Convention.

[19] Ibid.

[20] "Resolution Concerning War and Peace," 1940, at sbc.net. Copyright © 1999–2005 Southern Baptist Convention.

[21] "Resolution on Peace," May 1943, at sbc.net. Copyright © 1999–2005 Southern Baptist Convention.

[22] "Resolution on Peace of the World," 1948, at sbc.net. Copyright © 1999–2005 Southern Baptist Convention.

[23] Ibid.

borders. However, sometime during the second half of the twentieth century the Southern Baptist Convention shifted its position on this issue. In 1967, during the Vietnam War, the Convention called for a study of Scripture to find guiding principles when dealing with God-and-country issues.[24] In 1971 a similar resolution was passed.[25] Earlier the statements were quite confident of their position on the war issue. Now they wavered. Beginning in the 1980s resolutions were passed supporting a "strong national defense . . . as a deterrent to war."[26] In 1991 much praise was directed toward the military for its success in Desert Storm.[27] In 1994 a resolution commended those who participated in D-Day.[28] During the 1940s no similar commendation or expression of appreciation was adopted. In 1998 a surprising statement was made to the effect that "the purpose of military combat is to inflict deadly harm upon an enemy, and the essence of combat is to use force against an enemy in order to kill, damage or destroy—a purpose and essence aligned with the male role. . . ."[29] The resolution was in opposition to women serving in the military. The statement, however, seems to suggest that by nature men (males) are designed to "kill, damage, or destroy." A 2002 resolution of the Convention expressed support for the war on terror, a just war in their view, as undertaken by the government and the military.[30] The Southern Baptists never referred to any war as a just war prior to this statement. In 2003 the Southern Baptist Convention adopted a resolution supporting the war in Iraq, calling it also a just war.[31] In 2004 President George W. Bush addressed the Southern Baptist Convention and thanked them for their support of the war (Iraq).[32] In the same year the military was praised for "maintaining peace throughout the world."[33] There was

[24] "Resolution on Peace," June 1967, at sbc.net.

[25] "Resolution on World Peace," June 1971, at sbc. net.

[26] "Resolution on Peace and National Security," 1981, at sbc.net. Copyright © 1999–2005 Southern Baptist Convention.

[27] "Resolution on Operation Desert Storm," June 1991, at sbc.net.

[28] "Resolution on Commending World War II Veterans on the Occasion of the 50th Anniversary of D-Day," 1994, at sbc.net.

[29] "Resolution on Women in Combat," 1998, at sbc.net. Copyright © 1999–2005 Southern Baptist Convention.

[30] "On the War on Terrorism," 2002, at sbc.net.

[31] "On the Liberation of Iraq," 2003, at sbc.net.

[32] "Bush reiterates stance on key issues to Southern Baptists," by Erin Curry, a news release, June 15, 2004, at sbc.net. Copyright © 1999–2005 Southern Baptist Convention.

[33] "On Appreciation of Our American Military," 2004, at sbc.net. Copyright © 1999–2005 Southern Baptist Convention.

also an expression of "pride and strong support for our American military personnel."[34] The increasing support of war and the military in the Southern Baptist Convention partially explains the easy acceptance of the change in wording of the sixth commandment from "You shall not kill" to "You shall not murder."

African-American Baptists Against a War

African-American Baptists, by contrast, in the early twenty-first century took a strong and specific stand against the war in Iraq, but not on biblical or doctrinal grounds. Reflecting the influence of Dr. Martin Luther King, Jr., a prominent pastor and pacifist in their denomination, the National Baptists passed a resolution stating that they favor "non-violent social change and international peacemaking"[35] as a way to bring resolution to the Iraq problem.

"You shall not kill" in Pentecostalism

The history of pacifism in the Assemblies of God, an evangelical/ Pentecostal church, as traced by Murray W. Dempster, demonstrates that that denomination, though adopting a pacifist statement in 1917 and registering as a pacifist church, may not have been committed to pacifism at the grassroots. Citing the "you shall not kill" commandment and a number of other biblical texts, the Assemblies of God adopted a resolution in April of 1917 that stated: "we cannot conscientiously participate in war and armed resistance which involves the actual destruction of human life since this is contrary to our view of the clear teachings of the inspired Word of God, which is the sole basis of our faith."[36] According to Dempster the early pacifism was held only by a small group of men who managed to persuade the executives and General Council to pass the resolution. Their thinking was based on different and distinct ideas, among which were the desire to return to the Christianity of the early

---

[34] Ibid.

[35] "Resolution on Opposing War On the People of Iraq," Jan. 23, 2003. Website of the National Baptist Convention: www.nationalbaptist.com.

[36] Murray W. Dempster, "Pacifism in Pentecostalism: The Case of the Assemblies of God," in Jeffrey Gros and John D. Rempel, eds., *The Fragmentation of the Church and Its Unity in Peacemaking* (Grand Rapids: Eerdmans, 2001) 138.

church, which was pacifist, the recognition that war spawns evil not just within the war but in the way it affects society economically and socially, and the belief that it is wrong to kill someone for whom Christ died.[37] He argues that the statement represented a minority viewpoint, that most Assemblies of God people would not have been pacifists. Jay Beaman, however, while agreeing that members of the Assemblies of God were divided on the issue, points out that pacifist articles regularly appeared in periodicals of the Assemblies of God, that there was fervent support of conscientious objectors at a time when it was socially unacceptable to be pacifistic (during the first World War), and that steps were taken to become registered as an official pacifist denomination.[38] All of these point to support of the pacifist position by a larger number of leaders and not just a few on the fringe. Beaman further argues that "the strong biblical basis initially employed by the Assemblies of God to justify its pacifism may have proved to be a serious impediment to its later abandonment. . . . in the mid-1960s it was necessary for the Assemblies of God to reinterpret biblical texts regarding the taking of human life before the church could change its statement on pacifism, which it then did in 1968."[39] The 1917 statement itself offers support for pacifism only by quoting Scripture, including Exod 20:13. By the second half of the twentieth century and into the twenty-first century the Assemblies of God were no longer making pacifist statements. In regard to Exod 20:13 they state:

> In light of this, how are we to understand the sixth commandment: "You shall not murder" (Exodus 20:13)? The Hebrew word used here (*raisach*) in the ancient manuscripts is descriptive of an act of *willful* and *personal* vengeance. While the outcome may be similar to the killings of war, the motive and driving force are quite different. The language of Exodus 20:13 does not suggest that we are to disallow participation in war, even if that participation involves killing.[40]

And so the same text was used in the Assemblies of God to reject killing in war at the beginning of the twentieth century and and support it at the beginning of the twenty-first century. In his book, *Pentecostal Pacifism*,

[37] Ibid. 145, 148, 154–55.

[38] Jay Beaman, "Pacifism Among the Early Pentecostals," in Theron F. Schlabach and Richard T. Hughes, eds., *Proclaim Peace: Christian Pacifism from Unexpected Quarters* (Urbana: University of Illinois Press, 1997) 85–87.

[39] Ibid. 86.

[40] Website of the Assemblies of God under Assemblies of God Beliefs, Contemporary Issues, "War and Conscientious Objectors," at http://ag.org.

Jay Beaman lists many Pentecostal and holiness churches that were anti-war based upon a simple reading of Scripture. Most of these denominations followed the trajectory of the Assemblies of God and dropped that stance either de facto or in their official statements later on, with the notable exception of the Brethren in Christ.[41]

African-American Denominations and "You shall not kill"

Two predominantly African-American Pentecostal denominations, on the official level at least, had taken strong anti-killing stances in the first half of the twentieth century. Theodore Kornweibel writes that early in its twentieth-century history the Church of God in Christ expressed strong opposition to killing.[42] One of its early leaders, Bishop C. H. Mason, was put on trial for taking a pacifist position. An official doctrine of the Church of God in Christ that has never been rescinded states: "We believe the shedding of human blood or the taking of human life to be contrary to the teaching of our Lord and Saviour and as a body we are averse to war in all its various forms."[43] According to Kornweibel, however, like others of the evangelical churches, the Church of God in Christ ignored this doctrine in the second half of the twentieth century. In the first half of the century the Apostolic Church (Pentecostal Assemblies of the World, "PAW"), led by Bishop G. T. Haywood, adopted the following statement as Article 12:

> In time of persecution, or ill-treatment at the hands of an enemy we should not "avenge ourselves." But rather give place to wrath; for it is written, "Vengeance is mine; I will repay, saith the Lord." (Rom. 12:19; Deut. 32:35.) Neither shall we take up any weapon of destruction to slay another, whether in our own defense, or in the defense of others, for it is written, "Do violence to no man." (See Lu. 3:14; Matt.

[41] Jay Beaman, *Pentecostal Pacifism: the origin, development, and rejection of Pacific belief among the Pentecostals* (Hillsboro, KS: Center for Mennonite Brethren Studies, 1989). The Brethren-In-Christ Church is an Anabaptist, pietist, holiness denomination that emerged out of the Mennonite Church, one of the historic peace churches. It has maintained its pacifist stance.

[42] Theodore Kornweibel Jr., "Race and Conscientious Objection in World War I," in Schlabach and Hughes, eds., *Proclaim Peace.*

[43] First Ecclesiastical Jurisdiction, Southern California, Church of God in Christ, websitehttp://www.southerncal-cogic.org/believe.htm.

26:52; John 18:36; 15:18, 19.) We should rather suffer wrong than to do wrong.[44]

Article 13 continues this thought, specifically appealing to the "You shall not kill" commandment to support its position. It reads ". . . it is our duty to be in obedience to all requirements of the laws that are not contrary to the word of God, and that does not force one to the violation of the sixth commandment by bearing arms, or going to war."[45] Morris Golder's 1959 thesis on the doctrines of the Pentecostal Assemblies of the World does not mention pacifism as one of the doctrines of the church.[46] This is the period in history when the church began to soften its stance on the issue. Jane Sims, a pastor in the Pentecostal Assemblies of the World, notes that through the Second World War PAW men were conscientious objectors. They served in the military, but in noncombatant positions such as the medical corps. There were many sermons throughout that time that reiterated the pacifist position of the denomination. This changed during the Vietnam era. Pastors of that generation stopped preaching the peace position and young men entered the military when drafted and served in combatant positions. Part of the reason for the change was the influence of Martin Luther King, Jr. and the Civil Rights movement. The "turn the other cheek" theology was rejected by youth who took an activist stance in relation to race issues. This carried over into war issues.[47]

John Howard Yoder made a distinction between the pacifism of the historic peace churches and that of the early Pentecostal churches, which he saw as based on "the synergy of enthusiasm and prima facie Biblicism."[48] That Biblicism "did not mature into a solid ethical hermeneutic."[49] With regard to the Pentecostal churches, Beaman thinks that "pacifism is not a key ingredient in the self-understanding of these groups and their

---

[44] G. T. Haywood, *The Teachings of the Apostolic Church According to the Bible*, 6 Indianapolis, IN, no date, no publisher.

[45] Ibid. 6–7.

[46] Morris Ellis Golder, *A Doctrinal Study of the Pentecostal Assemblies of the World*. M.A. Thesis. Butler University, 1959. The only reference to war is a paraphrase of the last phrase of Isaiah 2:4 as a future event. Pentecostals believe that this future is about to unfold.

[47] Jane Sims, co-pastor at Calvary Community Church (PAW), Columbus, IN, telephone interview, July 27, 2004. Used by permission.

[48] Jay Beaman, *Pentecostal Pacifism*, iii.

[49] Ibid.

historians."[50] Therefore it was easy to drop it as some of the Pentecostal denominations entered the mainstream.

Evangelicals, the Military, and the Sixth Commandment

Anne C. Loveland has done the most complete research available into the relationship between evangelicals and the military during the second half of the twentieth century. According to Loveland evangelicals started to become heavily involved in the military after the Second World War. Evangelicals noticed that young men returning from military service had picked up negative behaviors such as drinking, cursing, and sexual promiscuity. These churches saw the military as a mission field, and they wanted to provide wholesome influences and wholesome leisure activities for the servicemen and women.[51] They encouraged evangelical clergy to become chaplains.[52] Ranking officers who proclaimed Christian faith became celebrities in evangelical circles. Since killing is at least a potential occupation of military personnel, how did evangelicals square that with their faith? Loveland notes that for many evangelicals "killing the enemy in combat was not murder and therefore did not violate the Sixth Commandment."[53] God and state were fused by evangelicals, who according to Loveland believed that obeying the government *was* obeying God[54] (Romans 13)—unless the government asked the Christian to do something contrary to God's will. An example of something contrary to the will of God would be prohibiting worship,[55] not killing people. In a 1955 article entitled "Is Pacifism Christian?" Gordon Clark joins the issues of capital punishment and war, arguing that a biblical defense of killing in capital punishment would also apply to war. He cites a text

[50] Ibid. 37.

[51] Anne C. Loveland, *American Evangelicals and the U.S. Military 1942–1993* (Baton Rouge: Louisiana State University Press, 1996).

[52] An ongoing issue among Southern Baptists and other evangelicals is perceived discrimination against evangelicals in the military chaplaincy. In 2003 a charge was made that the Navy continued to favor "liturgical" traditions even though evangelicals were more successful in drawing people into worship services. See resolutions, sbc.net.

[53] Loveland, *American Evangelicals,* 5, 157.

[54] Ibid. 127, 157.

[55] Ibid. 127.

that supporters of capital punishment frequently use, Gen 9:6,[56] "the one who sheds the blood of a human, by a human his [or her] blood will be shed." He adds that God commanded the Israelites to fight. Moreover, Jesus supported the payment of taxes. (Clark assumes that the taxes were used for war rather than Temple support) and Paul instructed Christians to obey the government because it was granted the "power of the sword" in Romans 13.[57] All of these texts, Clark believes, support killing. Doctrines that most evangelicals subscribe to, such as the universality of sin and pre-millennialism,[58] permit evangelicals to accept killing in war as inevitable.[59] The melding of evangelicalism, patriotism, and militarism was one factor that led to the easy acceptance of the change in the translation of the sixth commandment.

"You shall not kill" and
Capital Punishment Among the Evangelicals

Another issue that exercised evangelicals in the twentieth and twenty-first centuries was capital punishment. As a group conservative evangelicals favor the retention of capital punishment to a greater extent than the general public. One of the evangelical denominations, the Southern Baptist Convention, for the first time in its history adopted a resolution in support of capital punishment in the year 2000.[60] Evangelicals point to a number of biblical texts to support a pro-capital-punishment position. Genesis 9:6 in the *NIV* translation reads: "Whoever sheds the blood of man, by man shall his blood be shed; for in the image of God has God made man." This statement is read as an imperative and is interpreted to mean that anyone who kills another should, in turn, be killed by persons who have been granted the authority to do so by society. In an article published in the *Journal of the Evangelical Theological*

---

[56] Most evangelicals read this text as an imperative rather than a descriptive statement.

[57] Gordon H. Clark, "Is Pacifism Christian?" *United Evangelical Action*, August 1, 1955, pp. 5 and 23. This article was paired with one that defends pacifism.

[58] Premillennialism is a belief that there will be a heightened time of war and violence, the Tribulation, preceding the return of Christ. Then Christ will reign for a thousand-year period of peace.

[59] Loveland, *American Evangelicals*, 162–63.

[60] "On Capital Punishment," 2000, at sbc. net.

Society, James E. Priest wrote that "Nowhere in the Bible is the requirement of the death penalty more forcefully stated."[61] Priest goes on to explain that this requirement was placed under the rule of law in the Bible and later Talmudic discussion. This means that killing can only take place under the authority of the civil administrators. Killing by the civil administrators, as in capital punishment or war, is exempt from the sixth commandment. Popular evangelical writer Harold Lindsell makes this point in his 1973 book *The World, the Flesh and the Devil.* He writes: "There is no doubt that the Old Testament provides for both capital punishment and killing in wartime."[62] Continuing, he insists that Christians may not "use the commandment 'Thou shalt not kill' as substantive grounds for pacifism."[63] Other biblical arguments for the death penalty include Romans 13, the notion that the government has the right to "bear the sword," the assumption being that bearing the sword means killing people. Finally, evangelicals point to what they understand to be God's legislation of the death penalty in the Covenant Code (Exodus 21–23) and in ordering the Israelites to kill. For example, as translated by the *NIV,* Exod 21:17 reads: "Anyone who curses his father or mother must be put to death." Stanley J. Grenz explains that evangelicals understand Scripture to be a collection of "factual propositions."[64] The Bible, they believe, teaches both theological ideas and behavioral practices. The Christian searches the Scripture for guidance in life and for inspiration. In evangelical thinking, if the Bible says that a person committing a proscribed offense must be put to death, this applies to the contemporary era and not just to the community to whom the admonition was addressed in the ancient world. A "murder" rather than "kill" reading of the sixth commandment is more compatible with a pro-capital-punishment position.

Although evangelicals have "Thou shalt not kill" in their King James Bibles, most[65] have never understood the commandment to include killing in war, capital punishment, self-defense, or killing in police actions,

---

[61] James E. Priest, "Gen 9:6: A Comparative Study of Bloodshed in Bible and Talmud," *JETS* 31 (June 1988) 145.

[62] Harold Lindsell, *The World, the Flesh and the Devil* (Washington, DC: Canon Press, 1973) 84.

[63] Ibid. 95.

[64] Grenz, "Nurturing the Soul, Informing the Mind," 37.

[65] An exception would be evangelicals who fall under the Peace Church category, such as the Brethren in Christ, Brethren, Evangelical Friends, and some Mennonites. Usually churches in these traditions that identify themselves as evangelicals become estranged from their peace church heritage.

etc. The commandment is interpreted to mean that persons should not kill other persons illicitly, outside of the bounds of law. Nevertheless, evangelicals are not entirely of one mind on this position, as the following selection of reflections on the sixth commandment by influential evangelicals demonstrates.

Prominent Evangelical Voices on the Subject of "You shall not kill/murder"

Without question, the single most influential evangelical in the second half of the twentieth century was the evangelist Billy Graham. Over a period of decades Graham penned a newspaper column that was eventually syndicated across the country. He was frequently asked about the morality of Christian participation in war. The question was stated in this way: "Should a Christian participate in defense measures of war involving the use of weapons, considering that his purpose is to kill other children of God?"[66] In 1960 Graham responded that the purpose of war is not to "kill other children of God," but to "settle differences."[67] He goes on to say that citizens who cannot support their government should "take [their] citizenship elsewhere."[68] Although Graham does not speak directly to the "You shall not kill" commandment, his response implies that killing in war is not a violation.

The British evangelical John Stott is more cautious in his interpretation of Scripture for modern-day application. He notes that wars should not be defended based on texts from the Bible because "no nation can claim today to enjoy Israel's privileged position as a 'holy nation,' God's special covenant people, a unique theocracy."[69] Reading Romans 12 and 13 together, he concludes that two separate ethical systems are evident: an ethic for the individual and an ethic for the state. Unlike the individual, the state can punish "particular and identifiable people who have done wrong and need to be bought to justice."[70] He continues: "In the

[66] Billy Graham, *My Answer* (Garden City, NY: Doubleday, 1960) 178.

[67] Ibid.

[68] Ibid. A similar response is given in his 1988 book, a collection of newspaper column responses entitled *Answers to Life's Problems* (Minneapolis: Grayson, 1988). Ideologically he supports "just war" thinking. See ibid., 258.

[69] John Stott, *Decisive Issues Facing Christians Today* (Old Tappan, NJ: Fleming H. Revell Company, 1990) 88.

[70] Ibid. 90.

Old Testament the shedding of human blood was strictly forbidden except by specific divine sanction, i.e. in the execution of a murderer and in wars explicitly authorized by God."[71]

Elton Trueblood, an evangelical Quaker who was immensely influential in evangelical circles during his lifetime, wrote a book of reflections on the Ten Commandments. He clearly struggled with his pacifist Christian upbringing and the reality of the world wars through which he lived. He adopts the "murder" translation of the sixth commandment. He proposes that Christians should "cultivate an uneasy conscience concerning death. . . ."[72] Trueblood does not place absolute value on human life. He points out that people are going to die anyway. Wanton and careless killing of persons, however, leads to a devaluing of human life. Humans are to be valued because they are made in the image of God and are capable of relationship with God and others. He believes that sometimes killing is necessary but that Christians should be uneasy about killing others.

The highly successful 700 Club, similar to the secular talk shows with its variety of news, talk, and entertainment, presided over by its host, Pat Robertson, debuted in the mid-1960s and reigned supreme in evangelical Christian circles into the beginning of the twenty-first century. A child submitted a question to Robertson asking whether one "can be forgiven for killing another human being."[73] Robertson, a former Marine, answered the question about killing in war this way "if you go into battle in a just war . . . you may have to wound or even kill another human being who happens to be an enemy soldier coming against you."[74] Robertson quotes Rom 13:4 to support his position.

In 1975 two evangelicals from opposite ends of the spectrum in relation to killing in war and the "You shall not kill" commandment wrote companion articles for *Christianity Today*.[75] The first, "Can a Christian go to War?" by George W. Knight III, argued that the sixth commandment is limited to "murder." He cites Deuteronomy 20, where a list of rules for

[71] Ibid. 92.

[72] Elton Trueblood, *Foundations for Reconstruction* (rev. ed. New York: Harper & Brothers, 1061) 67.

[73] http://cbn.org/partners/bringiton/EthicalIssues.asp. This is the website of the 700 Club.

[74] Ibid.

[75] George W. Knight III, "Can a Christian Go to War?" *Christianity Today* 20 (Nov. 21, 1975) 4–7, and Myron Augsburger, "Beating Swords into Plowshares," *Christianity Today* 20 (Nov. 21, 1975) 7–9.

war is given. He points out that God instructs Israel to fight. There are even instructions to utterly destroy humans. Myron Augsburger, in an article titled "Beating Swords into Plowshares," argues against typical evangelical arguments in favor of war by pointing primarily to New Testament Scripture texts such as Romans 13, which he interprets to mean that God ordained government as a means to order society. He insists that the text is not saying that God ordains particular governments. He further argues that Christ is the one to whom loyalty is due above any government. In response to killing in the Hebrew Bible, he argues that biblical revelation is unfolding. As time goes on, people have a better understanding of what God desires. In 1980 a similar pairing of evangelical scholars with opposing views appeared under the article titles "Justice Is Something Worth Fighting For" by Robert D. Culver and "Why Christians Shouldn't Carry Swords" by John Drescher.[76] On this issue the magazine did not take a stand, but simply presented opposing viewpoints.

Stanley Hauerwas and William Willimon offer another interpretation of the sixth commandment. They suggest that it (along with the other commandments) is to be read not as a guideline for everyone, but only for people of faith. They see this commandment as "counter-cultural" and a critique of societal institutions. Affirming that "Murder is too limited a term to encapsulate the concern of this commandment,"[77] they interpret the sixth commandment as absolute in its position that human life (and maybe animal life) is never to be taken by another human. They find support for their position in the first chapter of Genesis, where in the creation narrative the absence of killing is to be the normal state of living beings. They point out that "killing in the Old Testament is not celebrated as good, but rather presented as a concession to our sin. As far as killing in the New Testament, it is exclusively done to Christians rather than by them, and nowhere is such killing, even if lawfully state-imposed . . . seen as positive."[78] (Hauerwas and Willimon seem to have forgotten that Jesus, who was not a Christian, is killed in the New Testament.) The two scholars realize that "in saying that God's people are not to take life, the commandment puts us at odds with every government

---

[76] Robert D. Culver, "Justice Is Something Worth Fighting For," and John Drescher, "Why Christians Shouldn't Carry Swords," *Christianity Today* 24 (Nov. 7, 1980) 14–23.

[77] Stanley M. Hauerwas and William H. Willimon, *The Truth About God* (Nashville: Abingdon, 1999) 80.

[78] Ibid. 90.

on earth."[79] In their thinking, the commandment is a critique of what governments and other power institutions do. Hauerwas and Willimon have taken a position at odds with most evangelicals, except those who count themselves as members of the so-called "Peace" churches: the Mennonites, the Brethren, and the Friends (Quakers).[80]

Other issues involving killing that evangelicals as a group tend to oppose include abortion, assisted suicide, and euthanasia. This is expressed by an oral retention of the traditional wording of the commandment.

Why "You shall not kill" Became "You shall not murder" in Evangelicalism

In the opinion of the author evangelicals easily accepted the kill-to-murder change for four reasons: an acceptance of the argument that the biblical word *rtsh* applied only to unlawful killings, the close connection (in the United States) between evangelicalism and militarism, a theology that firmly believes in an afterlife, placing belief above practice (believing in Jesus is more important than following the way of Jesus) and the mainstreaming of the evangelical community. One student of mine, whose name I no longer remember, made the startling statement in class that "It makes no difference whether you are alive or dead." He meant that if you are alive, you are with God. If you are dead, you are with God. This theology leads evangelicals to do extraordinary good (risking their own lives to spread the Gospel or tend to persons with communicable diseases), but it also leads to a devaluing of human life. Some strands of early evangelicalism, because they were counter-cultural, were also able to take a position on the sixth commandment that was counter-cultural but consistent with a plain reading of the biblical text. But as evangelicals entered the mainstream they developed a mainstream interpretation of the sixth commandment. However, evangelicals are changing because they are fully engaged in a post-modern world. Evangelicals are feeling a kinship with worldwide Christianity, particularly in developing nations in Africa and Asia where conservative forms of Christianity are the norm. These developments may make them less willing to identify so closely with any particular government.

[79] Ibid. 80.

[80] Not all Mennonites would consider themselves to be evangelicals. Certainly many Friends would also not consider themselves to be evangelicals.

Chapter 3

The Sixth Commandment
in the Mainline Traditions

The terminology "mainline" came into use in the early twentieth century to distinguish the long-established Protestant churches from those in the newer evangelical movements that were largely identified with fundamentalism[1] and Pentecostalism. Members of mainline denominations were heavily represented in the institutions of society, including the government, education, and the military. The role of religion in American society was largely shaped by the mainline denominations. The mainline churches, traditionally identified as the Presbyterian Church, U.S.A., the Episcopal Church, the Evangelical Lutheran Church in America, the American Baptists, the United Methodists, the Christian Church (Disciples of Christ), and the United Church of Christ, have long accepted the tenets and methodologies of critical Bible study. All identify the Bible as their foundational text, but beyond that they differ in the language they use to describe their understanding of the Bible itself and its role in Christian life today. None of these traditions has adopted a doctrine of inerrancy. Therefore they can more freely challenge traditional translations of biblical texts. The mainline denominations produced both the *Revised Standard Version (RSV)* in 1952 and the *New Revised Standard Version (NRSV)* in 1989. The *RSV* translated *rtsḥ* as "kill." The *NRSV* translated the same word as "murder."

---

[1] This association changes in the middle of the twentieth century when the neo-evangelicals emerge. See the chapter on evangelicals, above.

The State Church Traditions

The mainline denominations have a different socio-political history than the evangelical churches. That history influences how they translate and interpret biblical texts. The dominant mainline traditions trace their origins to state churches in Europe. The Episcopal Church is a daughter church of the Church of England. A revival movement within the Church of England spawned a new denomination that became the United Methodist Church. The Presbyterians descended from the Church of Scotland, which emerged as part of a Scottish (anti-English) identity movement. Lutheran Churches were state churches in Germany and Scandinavia. The UCC, which emerged in the twentieth century from Congregational roots, was never a state church, though the Congregational church, going back to the Puritans, wielded political power in colonial America. The political history of these denominations influences their interpretations of biblical texts, particularly those that relate to church and state, war and peace. Killing is something states do from time to time, and these denominations with state church roots have historically supported and justified those killings.

According to H. B. Clark, the Ten Commandments and other selections from the Bible formed the foundation of English law when they were adopted by King Alfred (ninth century C.E.).[2] The infusion of biblical law into English law and the political system led to a reinterpretation of the law to suit the needs of the state. One of the *raisons d'être* for the creation of a state is that there is a demonstrated need for protection from outside enemies. The commandment "You shall not kill" is reinterpreted to apply not to the state itself, but to private individuals who act against the will of the state.

Most of the mainline denominations in the late twentieth and early twenty-first century readily accepted a "murder" translation in the Ten Commandments. The argument these denominations use is that the Hebrew word *rtsh* is more properly understood as murder. However, behind the semantic argument is the pragmatic consideration that a murder reading allows for killings in which the state engages, such as war and capital punishment.[3]

---

[2] H. B. Clark, *Biblical Law* (Portland: Binfords & Mort, 1943; reprint Union, NJ: The Lawbook Exchange, 2001) 36.

[3] According to the literary context of Exodus 20 the Israelites have no political structure, certainly no state. These instructions are given to a loose collection of people

Although a major American mainline translation did not read "murder" until the publication of the *New Revised Standard Version* in 1989, the notion that *rtsḥ* really meant murder began appearing in commentaries and sermons much earlier. The *English Revised Version (ERV)*, published in 1885, translated "murder." The *ERV* was a revision of the King James Bible. American members of the *ERV* committee completed an American version of the *ERV* in 1901. It is known as the *American Standard Version (ASV)*. The *ASV* did not follow its British counterpart in changing the wording of the King James Bible for the sixth commandment. It retained "kill" in Exod 20:13.

What the Catechisms Teach

The catechism method of instruction (question and answer) is no longer dominant in mainline traditions. But the catechisms represent statements of what each denomination teaches about its core doctrines and beliefs, and so are still a good representative source of the official voice of a denomination. The catechisms were developed at a time when society was highly hierarchical, and they reflect that. Those in the privileged classes wanted to keep the established order. Explanations of the "You shall not kill" commandment that emerge in the catechisms enjoin the masses to maintain order among themselves and not harbor bad feelings or take action to harm neighbors or those higher up in the hierarchy. They do not reflect the harm or killing inflicted by the upper classes on the lower classes. That sensitivity develops later, when governments and church hierarchies become more democratic and the Social Gospel is in full swing.

Reading through the confessional statements and catechisms of the Presbyterian Church, U.S.A., one can follow its evolving thought on doctrines and ethical issues throughout the centuries. In the case of the Ten Commandments, official interpretations appear in the catechisms. The first catechism of the P.C.U.S.A. dates back to the sixteenth century and the Scottish church. It states that "You shall not kill" means "I am not to abuse, hate, injure, or kill my neighbor. . . ."[4] This broad understanding

---

who have in common only that they left Egypt and servitude together in order to craft a better life for themselves.

[4] *The Book of Confessions: the Presbyterian Church, U.S.A.* (Louisville: The Office of the General Assembly, 1991) 4.105.

of the commandment, however, is tempered by its application only to the individual as he or she makes personal choices. The "Larger Catechism" exempts war, self-defense, and capital punishment from the prohibitions falling under the kill commandment.[5] In 1998 the Presbyterian Church, U.S.A., produced a new study catechism that is also recognized by the United Church of Christ. In it the sixth commandment appears as "You shall not murder." The explanation accompanying the commandment reads, "God forbids anything that harms my neighbor unfairly. Murder or injury can be done not only by direct violence but also by an angry word or a clever plan, and not only by an individual but also by unjust social institutions. I should honor every human being, including my enemy, as a person made in God's image."[6] This statement holds social institutions accountable, a significant step away from the old hierarchical ethic.

In the catechism of the Episcopal Church the sixth commandment also appears with the "murder" translation. Avoiding specific issues of killing, the catechism says that the intent of the commandment is "to show respect for the life God has given us; to work and pray for peace; to bear no malice, prejudice, or hatred in our hearts; and to be kind to all the creatures of God."[7]

The catechism of the Evangelical Lutheran Church in America dates back to Martin Luther himself (sixteenth century). In the larger catechism as translated in the late 1990s, the fifth commandment in the Lutheran order reads "You are not to kill." Luther's catechism states that "neither God nor the government is included in this commandment."[8] Luther limits the application of the commandment to individuals. Reading through the lens of Matthew 5, he explains: "We must not kill, either by hand, heart, or word, by signs or gestures, or by aiding and abetting. It forbids anger, except . . . to persons who function in God's stead . . .

---

[5] *The Book of Confession: the Presbyterian Church, U.S.A.*, 7.246. "The Larger Catechism," according to Lorna Shoemaker, dates to 1647 (personal communication).

[6] Found on the website of the United Church of Christ under Faith, Ten Commandments: http://www.ucc.org/faith/presbycat.htm#TEN.

[7] The Catechism of the Episcopal Church, under The Ten Commandments, as found on the Episcopal Church website: http://www.mit.edu/~tb/anglican/intro/catechism.html.

[8] "The Ten Commandments" in the Larger Catechism, *The Book of Concord*, edited by Robert Kolb and Timothy J. Wengert, translated by Charles Arand, Eric Gritsch, Robert Kolb, William Russell, James Schaaf, Jane Strohl, and Timothy J. Wengert (Minneapolis: Fortress, 2000) 410.

that is, parents and governing authorities."[9] Luther also notes that the commandment is violated by those who could preserve the lives of others but fail to do so. He gives the example of someone who freezes to death because those who could have provided clothing did not.[10] Again the commandment is interpreted expansively, but it is limited to individual behavior.

Traditionally the Protestant Churches that became state churches exempted the state from the prohibition against killing. They supported wars (as long as they were just) and capital punishment. Toward the end of the twentieth century they produced the *New Revised Standard Version* Bible translation, which changed the wording of the commandment from "You shall not kill" to "You shall not murder."

The Social Gospel and the Interpretation of "You shall not kill"

During the late nineteenth and early twentieth centuries the Social Gospel movement was in its heyday, and it influenced interpretation of the "You shall not kill" commandment in mainline denominations. The Social Gospel movement grew up from the underside of society at a time and in a place where criticism of well-established institutions was rampant. The Social Gospel rejected a pie-in-the-sky-in-the-sweet-by-and-by theology in favor of an activist we-are-obligated-to-make-the-world-better-now theology. Interpretations of the "You shall not kill" commandment that emerged from this period show concern about industrialization and the negative effects it was having on the lives of the poor, particularly in the urban context. Pastors regularly condemned unsafe working conditions and unsafe housing. When people die on the job because they get caught in a machine, the employer has violated the "You shall not kill" commandment. When the lives of immigrants are slowly extinguished by tuberculosis and other diseases rampant in tenements because of crowding and inadequate ventilation, the landlords have violated the "You shall not kill" commandment. Along with these was a condemnation of alcohol abuse and smoking, which were called forms of suicide. Adulteration of milk and drugs were regularly condemned under this commandment because these practices led to the early demise of both

[9] "The Ten Commandments" *The Book of Concord*, 411.
[10] Ibid. 412.

children and adults. Another emerging concern of the period that was discussed under this commandment was the perceived refusal of some women to marry and bear children. This was referred to as race suicide.[11] Clovis Gillham Chappell was one of the few non-peace-church voices that thought war was condemned under the commandment.[12] In spite of the extreme sensitivity to the ways in which thoughtless behavior might bring about death directly and indirectly and the role of institutions in the death of individuals, few interpreters of the sixth commandment during the Social Gospel era considered the massive killings that take place under government sanction to be covered by it.

The *RSV* Translates "kill"; the *NRSV* Translates "murder"

Along with other Protestant denominations, mainline churches in the United States mostly used the King James Version in the first half of the twentieth century. The *Revised Standard Version (RSV)*, the translation of choice of mainline scholars and seminaries from the sixties through the eighties, was first published in 1952. The *Revised Standard Version* committee translated Exod 20:13 as "You shall not kill." A new committee was constituted to revise the *Revised Standard Version* in order to contemporize the language and more fully incorporate knowledge acquired from the Dead Sea Scrolls and other ancient manuscripts, which emerged just as the *RSV* was going to print. In the *New Revised Standard Version (NRSV,* 1990), Exod 20:13 became "You shall not murder," though no newly found manuscripts provided information that would suggest a change in the wording was needed. A textual note indicates that "kill" is an alternate translation. According to translator Patrick D. Miller, "the committee spent several hours in conversation and split down the middle when the vote came to decide between 'kill' and 'commit murder.'

---

[11] See William Masselink, *Sermons on the Commandments* (Grand Rapids: Zondervan, 1934); John Henderson Powell, Jr., *The Ten Commandments* (New York: Macmillan, 1932); Robert Henry Charles, *The Decalogue* (Edinburgh: T & T Clark, 1926); Robert Emory Golladay, *The Ten Commandments* (Columbus, OH: Lutheran Book Concern, 1915); Robert L. Ottley, *The Rule of Life and Love: An Exposition of the Ten Commandments* (London: R. Scott, 1913); James Oswald Dykes, *The Law of the Ten Words* (London: Hodder & Stoughton, 191?[sic]). Many others authors share similar sentiments in this period.

[12] Clovis Gillham Chappell, *Ten Rules for Living* (Nashville: Cokesbury, 1938) 94.

The chair had to cast the deciding vote."[13] Like the evangelicals who went against their usual practices in changing the wording from kill to murder, mainline scholars went against fundamental tenets of critical scholarship in order to translate "murder" where "kill" had previously appeared.

The deliberations around the wording of the sixth commandment in the *New Revised Standard Version* committee focused on the usage of the word *rtsh* in the book of Deuteronomy.[14] Because other texts suggest that God commanded the killing of people in war and capital punishment, the argument was made that Exod 20:13 cannot mean kill in general. This type of argumentation is usually rejected by critical scholars because they know that texts emerged in different contexts, with different audiences, addressing different cultural and historical situations. It is not at all unusual to have different opinions expressed on an issue within the Bible and even to have different opinions expressed in side-by-side texts. When faced with contradictory texts, the critical scholar first examines each text within its own context to determine meaning. Then the scholar moves to similar texts or, in the case of the study of a word, other texts where the word is used. Frequently scholars point out that Exodus 21 lists a number of situations in which the death penalty may be used. Its close proximity to Exodus 20 leads some to interpret Exodus 20 in light of Exodus 21. From a scholarly standpoint this is not appropriate. These two texts may have emerged, and probably did emerge, from entirely different sources. Evidence of this is found in the dissimilarities in the chapters. The genres of the two texts are not the same. One, Exodus 20, is classified as apodictic law, a general statement or command that is presented without sanctions. Exodus 21 is classified as casuistic or case law presented in the formula, "If a person does such and such, so and so will be the result." Moreover, the language of Exodus 21 is not the language of Exodus 20. The word in question, *rtsh*, does not appear in Exodus 21 at all. What does appear in Exodus 21 is the phrase "surely die." The person who does such and such will surely die. The crime that will result in the death of the victim is described as "striking down" rather than "killing." Further, the instructions do not specify that the community is to carry out the death sentence. It could mean and was

---

[13] Patrick D. Miller, "What Translation Is," SBL Forum at the SBL website: http://www.sbl-site.org/Article.aspx?ArticleId=93.

[14] Telephone interview with Dr. Walter Harrelson (*NRSV* translation team member), February 16, 2004.

traditionally interpreted in Judaism to mean that God would strike the person dead. It may also imply that the deed itself will come back upon the head of the doer.

To be sure, one may speak about the editor's theology in particular biblical texts. The editor may very well have intended the reader to form a consistent theology by placing certain texts side by side. But even the editorial streams of biblical texts were not of one accord.[15]

So if the methods of critical scholarship do not lead to a translation of murder, why did the mainline traditions revert to pre-modern scholarship methods to deal with the sixth commandment? People want to kill people, and they want biblical permission to do so. The translators of the *NRSV* and the other translations of the late twentieth century gave them that permission. Both lay people and scholars have been inculturated into the societies in which they live. Those who live in cultures that sanction killing in war and capital punishment are more likely to read the sixth commandment in a more limited way because it suits a culturally created worldview.

Non-State Church Mainline Traditions

Denominations that did not emerge as state churches were more likely to take the counter-cultural position of opposing killing, including killing in war, early in their history, basing their position on the sixth commandment and Matt 5:21-22, but this changed as they entered the mainstream of culture and society.

The Christian Church (Disciples of Christ) traces its origins to a series of revival meetings that culminated at Cain Ridge, Kentucky in the early years of the nineteenth century. The early Disciples were largely disgruntled Baptists and Presbyterians. The expression "no creed but Christ" summarizes the Disciple position of allowing each believer theological freedom. Disciples do not have to adhere to a particular set of beliefs to count themselves a member of this denomination. According to Michael Casey, early leaders of the Stone–Campbell movement were pacifists until the First World War, following the pattern of the early church.[16] Alexander Campbell, a founding leader, made an important

[15] See Chapter One above for further discussion of how to read biblical texts.

[16] Michael W. Casey, "Churches of Christ and WWII Civilian Public Service," in Theron F. Schlabach and Richard T. Hughes, eds., *Proclaim Peace* (Urbana: University of Illinois Press, 1997) 99.

speech in opposition to war in 1848. In the speech he did not address the commandment itself, but it obviously had relevance to his interpretation. He states that Israel could fight because it was a unique theocracy. Such a theocracy no longer exists; therefore no modern state can claim to kill on behalf of God or under God's authority. Interestingly enough, what Michael Casey calls the more "sectarian" groups of the Christian Churches, such as those who adhered to "one-cup" or "nonclass" positions, were more likely to hold to a pacifist position during the First and Second World War than mainline Disciples of Christ.[17] In an essay on capital punishment Campbell reflected directly on the sixth commandment. He writes: "It has been said, not by those of old time, but by those of our time, that the sixth precept of the Decalogue, 'Thou shalt not kill,' inhibits all taking of human life. A sect of extreme pietists on Long Island, it is reported, gave to the precept a broader interpretation, and forbade the killing of any living creature for food. They are as consistent as he who says the precept *'thou shalt not kill'* prohibits capital punishment. It is the very precept which calls for the blood of him that violates it."[18] Campbell notes in support of capital punishment that on the very day that Moses delivered the Ten Commandments he ordered the killing of three thousand idolaters.[19] Campbell is atypical in that most people who apply the commandment to war also apply it to capital punishment.

The American Baptist Church (ABC) is a new name for an older denomination formerly known as the Northern Baptist Church. The name was changed in 1950. The Northern Baptist Church split from its southern counterpart during the American Civil War. The ABC describes Scripture as "the most authoritative guide to knowing and serving the triune God."[20] As Northern Baptists (1922) they took a determined anti-war stance. They affirmed that war is "contrary to every Christian ideal and teaching."[21] American Baptists in the second half of the twentieth century adopted a number of resolutions advising governments on foreign policy issues related to avoiding war. Just war criteria are not cited, and

[17] Ibid. 100. One-cup means using only one cup in communion services rather than individual cups. Nonclass refers to groups opposed to Sunday school.

[18] "Is Capital Punishment Sanctioned by Divine Authority?" in Alexander Campbell, *Popular Lectures and Addresses* (Philadelphia: James Challen and Son, 1863) 334.

[19] Ibid. Campbell is referring to the golden calf incident related in Exodus 32.

[20] At www.abc-usa.org, under "Who we are" and then "Our commitment to the Bible."

[21] "American Baptist Resolution on the Abolition of War," 1922, reaffirmed in 1987, at www.abc-usa.org

Scripture is not quoted. Resolutions in opposition to capital punishment were adopted in the 1950s and 1960s and reaffirmed in the 1980s,[22] but the ABC does not have a denomination-specific interpretation of the sixth commandment.

The United Methodist Church both in its earlier incarnations (as, for example, the Methodist Episcopal Church) and its current one has been active in social issues. The church has recently taken a strong anti-war stance. The Social Discipline of the UMC reads, in language remarkably similar to a resolution adopted by the Southern Baptists a half century earlier, "We believe war is incompatible with the teachings and example of Christ."[23] It goes on to confess that some in the denomination take an absolute stance against war while others believe that it is appropriate to resort to war when in situations of "unchecked aggression, tyranny and genocide."[24] The United Methodist Statement of Faith does not speak specifically to the "You shall not kill" commandment.

Interpretations of the Sixth Commandment by Mainline Scholars and Those Who Have Been Influential in Mainline Circles

In 1824 Archbishop of Canterbury Thomas Secker used the "murder" translation in his book *Discourses on the Commandments, and the Sacraments of Baptism and the Lord's Supper.* He defines murder as "taking away a person's life, with design, and without authority. Unless both concur, it doth not deserve that name."[25] He further explains that persons can murder themselves through "adventurous rashness, by ungoverned passion, by an immoderate anxiety, or by an obstinate or careless neglect of his own preservation. . . ."[26] Secker believed that the sixth com-

---

[22] "Resolution on Capital Punishment," reference number 8064:3182 on the American Baptist website under "Policy Statements and Resolutions," at http://www.abc-usa.org/resources/resol/cappun.html.

[23] The social principles of the *Book of Discipline of the United Methodist Church*, 2000, Paragraph 165 C, on their website at http://www.unitedmethodist.org/war_03.html.

[24] "Military Service," under "Social Principles," in *The Book of Discipline of the United Methodist Church*, paragraph 164G.

[25] Thomas Secker, *Discourses on the Commandments, and the Sacraments of Baptism and the Lord's Supper* (Philadelphia: S. Potter & Co., 1824) 77.

[26] Ibid. 85.

mandment, however, allowed for an equally broad interpretation of permissible killing. It allowed for self-defense (including war as a kind of self-defense), capital punishment both by "magistrates" and "private persons," because "this is only another sort of self defence, defending the public from what also would be pernicious to it. . . ."[27] Allowable warfare, in his thinking, is not limited to self defense but also includes wars "to obtain redress of injuries. . . ."[28] This goes beyond "just war" criteria, which usually allow war only for self-defense.

Harold Flowers expressed more uneasiness with traditional interpretations of the commandment than others of his generation. He noted that "deaths due to deliberate violence are extremely rare. . . . But what our conscience and sentiment need to be educated against is that criminal ignorance and neglect which is so often destructive of health and life."[29] Flowers then lists a variety of social ills, from unsafe working conditions to slum housing. He contrasts what he refers to as primitive practices to civilization. Although there is a list of "capital punishment" cases in Exodus 21, he rejects most of them because the punishment is too severe for the crime. He notes that the ancient Israelites did not always execute people for the crimes listed there. In many cultures, including Israel, fines were substituted for eye-for-an-eye justice. He implies that even in the case of those things that most people think limit the scope of the commandment, civilization allows other ways of dealing with offenses.

The twentieth-century biblical scholar Martin Noth concluded that the verb made "no distinction between premeditated murder and unpremeditated killing, but both . . . include the concept of the arbitrary."[30] He writes that "it was customary in Hebrew for other expressions to be used both for the execution of the death penalty imposed by legitimate trial and for the killing of an enemy in war. . . ."[31]

Noth's contemporary Brevard Childs argued that the meaning of the Hebrew word used in the commandment changed over time. The earlier meaning represented in Numbers 35 was associated with blood revenge. The later meaning prohibited "acts of violence against a person which

[27] Ibid. 78.

[28] Ibid.

[29] Harold Joseph Flowers, *The Permanent Value of the Ten Commandments* (London: G. Allen & Unwin, 1927) 183–84.

[30] Martin Noth, *Exodus* (Philadelphia: Westminster, 1962) 165.

[31] Ibid.

arose from personal feelings of hatred and malice."[32] He cites several texts, including Prov 22:13, where the imaginary lion attacks. That particular text, of course, cannot be interpreted to mean that the lion attacked out of "hatred or malice." Animals only attack because they feel threatened or are hungry.

Terrence Fretheim uses the translation "kill" because it "serves the community of faith best, forcing continual reflection on the meaning of the commandment and reminding all that in the taking of human life for any reason *one acts in God's stead,* in the face of which there should be a lengthy pause filled with careful soul-searching and the absence of vengefulness and arrogance. . . ."[33] Fretheim agrees with Childs that the word meaning of the Hebrew word *rtsḥ* probably changed over time, but it still has a broader range than that conveyed by the English word "murder." Killing, even legal killing, he argues, "should be very rare indeed."[34]

In 1986 Rodney Ring in a brief essay titled "The Bible Does Not Say 'thou shalt not kill,'" traces the "kill" translation to Martin Luther, who he claims was "influenced . . . by the New Testament."[35] He insists that he "allowed his (noble) Christian views to intrude into the Old Testament. . . ."[36] A number of commentaries written by Christians follow this line of reasoning. They understand "kill" in Exod 20:13 to have a more limited meaning. They then defend a broader ethic based on New Testament texts, though few repudiate all killing of human beings.

An interesting development in both the evangelical and mainline traditions is the broadening of the understanding of the word "kill" while a narrower definition for the commandment itself is retained. Most appeal to the Sermon on the Mount, though some notice that Leviticus 19 also contains statements about loving the stranger and not hating kin.

William Barclay is difficult to classify by tradition because he was an independent thinker, yet his writings were popular in both evangelical and mainline churches. Barclay held to the "kill" translation, concluding that it includes war. He expands the prohibition. Employers are guilty of murder when they provide unsafe working conditions. Landlords are guilty of murder when they rent out substandard housing that leads to

---

[32] Brevard S. Childs, *The Book of Exodus* (Philadelphia: Westminster, 1974) 421. See also John Newsom, *Exodus* (Louisville: Geneva Press, 1998).

[33] Terrence E. Fretheim, *Exodus* (Louisville: John Knox, 1991) 233.

[34] Ibid.

[35] Rodney Ring, "The Bible Does Not Say 'thou shalt not kill,'" *Dialog* 25 (1986) 310.

[36] Ibid.

the death of the poor (lead paint, no heat, fragile balconies, no fire escapes, etc.).[37] Barclay, however, in reflecting on the Ten Commandments appeals to the New Testament for support of this reasoning. He cites Jesus' "love your enemies," Jesus' own example of non-retaliation, and the idea that punishment should be for reformation.[38]

Walter Harrelson, one of the translators of the *New Revised Standard Version*, strongly supports the "kill" translation for Exod 20:13. He explains his position in his book, *The Ten Commandments and Human Rights*. He interprets the commandment as "You shall not take the life of your neighbor."[39] He bases this interpretation on the premise that "life belongs to God,"[40] and concludes that "the commandment not to take the life of a fellow human being is intended . . . to be precisely as broad as it is."[41] He bases this on the observation that the character of the commandment (and the rest of the Decalogue) is fundamentally different from that of other rules and regulations found in the Torah. This commandment, in his thinking, is not meant to prohibit killing by the community in, for example, war or capital punishment, but stresses the value of human life and reminds the community "that life belongs to God."[42] Humans may take life in war or capital punishment only when they are "acting directly on behalf of God."[43] A guiding principle is that life may be taken by the community only "in order to preserve life."[44] A murderer who may murder again may be subject to execution by the community. However, when other alternatives are available such as life imprisonment, for example, instead of the death penalty, or peaceful alternatives to war, they should be pursued.[45]

---

[37] Nineteenth-century evangelist Dwight L. Moody excludes war, capital punishment, and suicide but otherwise broadens the commandment in a similar way. By way of illustration he recalls the case of a son who tore up his mother's letters, knowing that they contained warnings against gambling and drinking. Moody says that son is murdering his mother. Dwight L. Moody, *On the Ten Commandments* (Chicago: Moody Press, 1896) 78.

[38] William Barclay, *The Old Law and the New Law* (Philadelphia: Westminster, 1972) 28–31.

[39] Walter Harrelson, *The Ten Commandments and Human Rights* (Macon, GA: Mercer University Press, 1997) 89.

[40] Ibid. 91.

[41] Ibid. 94.

[42] Ibid. 97.

[43] Ibid. 100.

[44] Ibid. 101.

[45] Ibid. 96–101.

J. Phillip Hyatt limits the prohibition to murder, but notes: "this meaning is not specifically derived from the verb employed."[46] He notes that the commandment was broadened not in the Bible but in history, to include war and capital punishment.[47]

Ronald Clements limits *rtsḥ* to "premeditated murder, and also to the private taking of revenge on people suspected of murder without recourse to proper legal investigation and public trial."[48]

Dale Patrick, a specialist in biblical law, supports the more generalized translation "kill" in Exod 20:13, noting that it is used more broadly in the Hebrew Bible. He observes that this commandment "covers lesser crimes as well . . . any act of violence . . . that might result in death."[49] He points to Leviticus 19 and the prohibition against hate and taking vengeance. Like Harrelson, Patrick does not think that the commandment "rules out participation in war or capital punishment"[50] when these are authorized by God. J. Gerald Janzen expresses similar views.[51]

Godfrey Ashby's treatment of the commandment tries to have it both ways. He limits the biblical meaning of *rtsḥ* to murder, "the slaying of personal, family or clan enemies; to the settling of old scores; and to the pursuit of vendettas and feuds."[52] But he broadens it for hermeneutical purposes to include state sponsored terrorism and "ethnic cleansing." The problem with these latter two is that actions taken legally by a state are not considered to be murder. Ashby broadens the definition of the English word murder beyond its typical usage in British and American law.

Cornelius Houtman notes that there is no object stated in the commandment. This is true of the other community-centered commandments as well. He thinks that the commandment speaks of "deliberate, violent and unlawful killing."[53] He also notes: "It is possible that the prohibition also pertains to indirect manslaughter as the result of intrigues or a-social conduct. . . ."[54] Houtman further suggests that the negative

---

[46] J. Philip Hyatt, *Exodus* (Grand Rapids: Eerdmans, 1971) 214.

[47] Ibid. 214.

[48] Ronald E. Clements, *Exodus* (Grand Rapids: Eerdmans, 1971) 125.

[49] Dale Patrick, *Old Testament Law* (Atlanta: John Knox, 1985) 53.

[50] Ibid.

[51] J. Gerald Janzen, *Exodus* (Louisville: Westminster John Knox, 1997) 150.

[52] Godfrey Ashby, *Go Out and Meet God: A Commentary on the Book of Exodus* (Grand Rapids: Eerdmans, 1998) 92.

[53] Cornelius Houtman, *Exodus,* tr. Sierd Woudstra (Leuven: Peeters, 2000) 60.

[54] Ibid.

and limited commandment is restated in positive and broad terms in the injunctions to love the neighbor as found in Leviticus 19 and Matthew 22.[55]

The mainline traditions on the whole have supported a "murder" translation in Exod 20:13 only since the second half of the twentieth century. A smattering of commentators used "murder" earlier than that, but a wholesale defection from "kill" only occurred with the publication of the *New Revised Standard Version*. Although many persons involved in the translation of this and other versions would argue that they became convinced that murder is the better translation based on etymological considerations, they were undoubtedly influenced by their cultural context, the history of their traditions, and personal commitments. In the end the mainline denominations changed the wording to express the theological conviction they have, in fact, consistently maintained since their days as state churches and churches of the cultural mainstream. Killing is prohibited only as a private act of an individual functioning against the tenets of the law or an act of a group that is functioning independent of government control (such as terrorists).

[55] Ibid. 61.

Chapter 4

The Sixth Commandment in Judaism

For more than two millennia, since the beginning of the Common Era, the text of the Torah (Genesis, Exodus, Leviticus, Numbers, and Deuteronomy) in the original language, Hebrew, has been carefully hand copied by specially trained Jewish scribes. In order to prevent corruption to the words of the text[1] the scribes used numerous safeguards. Words and letters were counted. Multiple appearances of the same word as well as errors believed to have been committed by earlier scribes were noted and, if needed, corrected in marginal notes. Thus a text of the Torah was well preserved.

Several Text Traditions of the Torah

In the years before the Common Era there were several versions of the Torah that differed somewhat from one another. The Hebrew Bible we use today represents one text tradition. The Septuagint, a Greek translation that had at its base a variant Hebrew text, was used by Greek-speaking Jews in the Levant (or Middle East) during the Hellenistic and Roman periods. Although the Septuagint was the product of Jewish translators, it fell out of favor in the Jewish community when it became

---

[1] The scribes counted words, letters, noted the mid-point of books or the number of repetitions of a word, added the masorah (vowel points, accent marks, commentary, etc.) to ensure the integrity of the text.

the text of choice in the early Christian community. The third text tradition, the Samaritan Pentateuch, was and is the sacred text of the small Samaritan community that inhabits the hill country surrounding Mount Gerizim. The Samaritans were also descendants of Israelite tribes. These three text traditions are still extant. Other variations on portions of the traditional texts were found among the Dead Sea Scrolls.

The Place of the Torah in Judaism

Animal sacrifice, libations, grain and incense offerings were important elements in the worship of ancient Israel. That form of worship, however, came to be restricted to temples and eventually to one temple in Jerusalem. Crises such as the dispersion of the Jews, social and political forces, and popular religion created synagogues, which were localized and responsive to the religious needs of ordinary people. Avigdor Shinan writes that with the development of the synagogues the Torah and Torah readings took on added significance. They were thought to "contain God's revelation for all time."[2] Through Torah, "God's voice" could be heard.[3]

According to Jordan Penkower, the Jewish sages believed that "there was one accurate text"[4] of the Torah, though they recognized that variants existed. Among the Dead Sea Scrolls, which date as far back as 200 B.C.E., are biblical texts that are virtually the same as the unpointed Masoretic[5] text that is used in synagogues today. For religious Jews the Torah (written and oral) is a sacred text. Penkower cites a source that affirms the power and significance of the Torah in Jewish thought this way: "even one letter added or omitted can destroy the world."[6] The "text" is the Hebrew and

[2] Avigdor Shinan, "The Bible in the Synagogue," *The Jewish Study Bible* (Oxford: Oxford University Press, 2004) 1929.

[3] Ibid.

[4] Jordan S. Penkower, "The Development of the Masoretic Bible," *The Jewish Study Bible*, 2078.

[5] The Masoretic text is one that includes vowel pointing, accent marks, and other additional material. The original biblical manuscripts did not include these. They only had consonants to represent words or phrases. The scrolls from which the Torah text is read in synagogues do not have the Masoretic markings. When the scrolls are read, however, it is with the memorized Masoretic markings. In addition to the texts that matched in biblical readings, texts with variant readings were also found.

[6] Jordan S. Penknower, "The Development of the Masoretic Bible," *The Jewish Study Bible*, 2078. He cites *b. ʿEruv.* 13a/*Sot.* 20a.

Aramaic Scripture. Not all Jews share the religiosity of the Orthodox, but the Bible nevertheless plays a role in the lives of many Reform, Conservative, Reconstructionist, and secular Jews as well. Jonathan and Nahum Sarna call the Bible "a living force . . . from which the structure of values to which Judaism subscribes ultimately derives."[7] They note that Reform Jews find "ethical exemplars" in the Torah and the prophetic tradition for both "Jews and non-Jews."[8] Zionists, even agnostic or atheistic Zionists, they observe, "turned to the Bible for inspiration and ideological justification."[9] Often the words inspiration and authority are paired when speaking of the Bible; however, they need not be. One may be inspired by biblical texts without considering them to be an authority for one's own faith or practice. The Sarnas imply that the Bible is an authority for religious Jews,[10] but not necessarily for others. Marc Zvi Brettler adds that the "canonical status of a book . . . has to do with the community's views of their centrality, authority, sacredness and inspiration."[11] These elements were thought to be present in the books contained in the Jewish Bible, which is why they are there. It is the community's recognition of the special character of these books that grants them canonical status. In an essay on "The Bible in Israeli Life," Uriel Simon observes that in the contemporary secular Israeli community "appeals to the Bible for inspiration or motivation are rare indeed. . . ."[12] However, the Bible retains its traditional importance in the lives of religious Jews. He makes a distinction between the written Torah[13] and the Talmud,[14] a later collection of Jewish writings that interpret and contextualize the Torah for Jews.

[7] Jonathan D. Sarna and Nahum M. Sarna, "Jewish Bible Scholarship and Translations in the United States," in Ernest S. Frerichs, ed., *The Bible and Bibles in America* (Atlanta: Scholars, 1988) 84. They specify that by "Jews" they mean both religious and secular Jews who so self-identify.

[8] Ibid. 104.

[9] Ibid.

[10] Ibid. 83–84.

[11] March Zvi Brettler, "The Canonization of the Bible," *The Jewish Study Bible,* 2075.

[12] Uriel Simon, "The Bible in Israeli Life," *The Jewish Study Bible,* 1996.

[13] The word *torah* means instruction. With a capital T it refers to the first five books of the Bible or sometimes to the Bible as a whole. In its broadest usage it refers to all the written and oral instruction given, in traditional understanding, by God to the people of Israel.

[14] Orthodox Jews believe that the Talmud contains instruction that was spoken by God at Sinai and passed on from generation to generation orally until it was written down to form the base text of the Talmud. There are two versions of the Talmud, the Babylonian Talmud and the Jerusalem Talmud.

He writes, "The Talmudic worldview considers the written law first in sanctity but not in authority. That privilege is reserved for the oral law, now found in the Talmud, which as the authoritative interpretation of the Bible, also determines which of its contents are effective today."[15] The Jerusalem Talmud itself does not specifically cite the sixth commandment in any discussion of biblical texts.[16]

Although English translations of the Bible do not have the status of the Hebrew and Aramaic text in Judaism, understanding the text is important to Jews. The text cannot provide insight, moral and ethical guidance, if it is not understood. This means that the Bible had to be translated into vernacular languages, and it was, going back to the Targums (Scripture texts and paraphrases written in Aramaic) and early Greek translations. Translations, however, are only approximations of the original texts, as the adage "translation is interpretation" reminds us. The translator has a particular point of view on an ethical or moral issue that is bound to come out in the translation.

Nearly every synagogue has a representation of the Ten Commandments etched into its building and/or listed in verbal or representative form on the cover of its Torah scrolls or at the front of the pulpit area. The Ten Commandments have become a symbol of Torah and Judaism in the West. But they are more than a symbol. They are one among many sets of ethical guidelines that direct the behavior, beliefs, and daily life of the Jewish community.

Jewish Translations of the Word *rtsḥ*

In most synagogues the words of the Torah are read in Hebrew each week regardless of the vernacular language in a particular place. Observant Jews, and even less-observant Jews, learn some Hebrew in order to follow the synagogue service.

Although Jews have been translating the Torah for over two thousand years, English translations of the Tanakh[17] appeared fairly late in translation history. The earliest Torah translation undertaken by a Jew appeared only in the middle of the nineteenth century. Whereas in Christianity the

---

[15] Simon, "The Bible in Israeli Life," 1996.

[16] Roger Brooks, *The Spirit of the Ten Commandments: Shattering the Myth of Rabbinic Legalism* (San Francisco: Harper & Row, 1990) 46.

[17] The Tanakh is the collection of books that Christians call the "Old Testament."

sixth commandment has been translated in popular American English Bibles as "You shall not murder" only in the last half of the twentieth century, this wording has a longer history in Judaism, though it is not an unchallenged reading. The 1917 English translation of the Bible published by the Jewish Publication Society reads "Thou shalt not murder."[18] According to Sarna the translators of the next significant translation of the Bible for Jews, the *TANAKH,* noted that it is an idiomatic translation that focused on "the deeper meaning . . . in contradistinction to the sur-face meaning, which they in some cases felt free to ignore"[19] because a "word-for-word translation did violence to the spirit of the Hebrew original."[20] First published in 1962,[21] the Torah portion of the *TANAKH* also uses the word "murder."[22] Everett Fox's idiosyncratic translation of the Torah reads "you are not to murder,"[23] but a note indicates: "Some interpreters view this as 'killing' in general. . . ."[24] In *The Bible as It Was,* James Kugel uses the "murder" translation, but adds "kill" as an alternate reading. He explains that the parameters covered by the commandment are not specified.[25] The "murder" translation has not been consistent in the history of Judaism.

Isaac Leeser's 1853 translation of the Bible for English-speaking Jews reads "Thou shalt not kill."[26] The Leeser translation was influenced by the King James version. This is evident in the use of archaic language and phrases taken wholesale from it. Leeser's goal was to correct the King James version according to Jewish interpretations of Scripture. He changed "virgin" to "young woman" in Isa 7:14, but he did not change "kill" to "murder" in Exod 20:13.[27] The Spanish Jewish translation *Humas*

---

[18] Philadelphia: Jewish Publication Society, 1917.

[19] Sarna, "Jewish Bible Scholarship and Translations in the United States," 109.

[20] Ibid.

[21] *TANAKH: The Holy Scriptures* (Philadelphia: The Jewish Publication Society, 1988) 116.

[22] Everett Fox concurs. Everett Fox, *The Five Books of Moses* (Dallas: Word Books, 1995).

[23] Ibid. 372.

[24] Ibid. 372, n. 13.

[25] James L. Kugel, *The Bible as It Was* (Cambridge, MA: The Belknap Press of Harvard University Press, 1998) 383–84.

[26] Isaac Leeser, *The Twenty-four Books of the Holy Scriptures* (Philadelphia: Shermoan & Co., 1853) 106.

[27] David Levi, responding to a series of letters written by Joseph Priestley, uses the word "murder" in his list of prohibitions as stated in the Noahide laws. Presumably he would have used the same word in the Ten Commandments. See Joseph Priestley,

de Parasioth y Aftharoth, published in 1627, reads *"No mates."* Mates means "kill," not murder. The Targum Onkelos, written in the ancient Aramaic language, reads לא תקתול נפֿש, "You shall not kill a person [or a life, or a soul]."[28] The verb used is *qtl*, not *rtsh* (the word used in Exod 20:13). It means "kill" in general. The chosen word in the Septuagint, the early Jewish translation of the Bible into Greek, is φονεύσεις,[29] which can mean "murder," but also simply "kill." One Greek Septuagint concordance uses the Latin word *occido*, which means "kill," to translate both the Hebrew word רצח and the Greek word φονεύσεις.[30] The first-century Jewish historian Josephus uses a form of the Greek word found in the Septuagint.[31] The Jewish philosopher Philo, however, chooses the word ἀνδροφονεῖν, "human-slayer," in a phrase referring to the commandment.[32] The Nash papyrus, a first-century Hebrew fragment that lists the Ten Commandments, has the same words that appear in Exod 20:13 for the sixth commandment, לוא תרצח.[33] From these few examples it is clear that the commandment has not always been interpreted to mean "murder," and only "murder," in the Jewish tradition.

Where Did the Idea Emerge
That *rtsh* Only Means Murder?

So, from where does the "murder" translation arise? The distinguished biblical scholar Nahum Sarna comments that Rashbam and Bekhor Shor,

Letters to the Jews ([New York]: Birmingham-printed. New-York: reprinted by J. Harrisson, for B. Gomez, bookseller and stationer, no. 97, Maiden-Lane, 1794), "Letters to Dr. Priestley," 66.

[28] *The Bible in Aramaic* 1, "Pentateuch" (Targum Onkelos) (Leiden: Brill, 1959) 122.

[29] *The Greek Septuagint Version* (London: Samuel Bagster, n.d., 1884?).

[30] *Concordantiae Graecae in Septuaginta Interpretes* 2 (Amstelodam Et Trajecti Ad Rhenum, 1718) 644 and 117 (Hebrew Index).

[31] *Josephus in Nine Volumes: IV: Jewish Antiquities*, tr. Henry St. John Thackeray, M.A. (Cambridge, MA: Harvard University Press, 1930; repr. 1978) 3:91–92 (pp. 360–61).

[32] *Philo in Ten Volumes (and two supplementary volumes)*, tr. F. H. Colson, M.A. (Cambridge, MA: Harvard University Press, 1937, repr. 1968) 7:72–73. According to Richard A. Freund, Philo and the Nash Papyrus have a different ordering of the verses of the three commandments: "adultery, murder, stealing." See his "The Decalogue in Judaism and Christianity," in Craig A. Evans and James A. Sanders, eds., *The Function of Scripture in Early Jewish and Christian Tradition*, (Sheffield: Sheffield Academic Press, 1998) 131.

[33] "The Hebrew Papyrus of the Ten Commandments," *JQR* 15 (1903) (repr. New York: Ktav, 1966) 395.

twelfth-century French rabbis, state that the root *rtsh* is used only for "illegal killing."[34] Martin Lockshin agrees, but points out that Rashbam was incorrect in the example he used. Rashbam cited Num 35:16 and Deut 4:42 as support for his belief that *rtsh* means "murder." In the Numbers verse the killer "strikes him and he dies." The word describing the deed is not *rtsh*, the word used in the sixth commandment. The Numbers text describes an unintentional killing, not murder. In neither case was Rashbam correct. Lockshin comments "Rashbam's claim, then, that the verb רצח describes only unjustified homicide seems difficult to sustain."[35] Indeed, it is impossible to sustain, as Chapter One of this book demonstrates.

Jewish Interpretations of the Sixth Commandment

Benno Jacob's exposition on Exod 20:13 understands the commandment to permit "justified executions" whether in self-defense or in societal self-defense. He wrote that "you shall not murder" is "the correlative of the drive to preserve one's own life,"[36] and he thinks that the word intends to insist upon "Respect even for the lives of strangers . . . ." Hence the commandment extends beyond the community of Israel.

W. Gunther Plaut, in his commentary on the book of Exodus, writes that *rtsh* refers to "unauthorized homicide," noting that "the penalty for murder is given in Exod 21:12."[37] He believes that the "kill" translation is too broad and that neither killing in war nor capital punishment is included in the prohibition.

Jeffrey Tigay, in the *Jewish Study Bible*, agrees with Plaut. He argues that some forms of killing are permitted in the Hebrew Bible and therefore this commandment cannot be a general prohibition against killing.[38]

---

[34] Nahum Sarna, *Exodus*. JPS Torah Commentary (Philadelphia: The Jewish Publication Society, 1991) 113. On Bekhor Shor see also Moshe Greenberg, "The Tradition Critically Examined," in Ben-Zion Segal, ed., *The Ten Commandments in History and Tradition*. English ed. by Gershon Levi (Jerusalem: Magnes Press, 1990) 104.

[35] *Rashbam's Commentary on Exodus*, edited and Translated by Martin I. Lockshin (Atlanta: Scholars, 1997) 218; see also 217.

[36] *The Second Book of the Bible, interpreted by Rabbi Benno Jacob*, tr. Walter Jacob in association with Yaakov Elmon (Hoboken, NJ: Ktav, 1992) 572. The first draft of this book was completed in 1940. Editing continued into the following decade.

[37] W. Gunther Plaut, *The Torah: A Modern Commentary* (New York: Union of American Hebrew Congregations, 1981) 554. The word *rtsh* does not appear in Exod 21:12.

[38] Jeffrey H. Togay, "Exodus," *The Jewish Study Bible*, 150.

Barry Cytron observes that in the Jewish tradition there was, over the centuries, an attempt to understand the meaning of a "do not kill" commandment in the light of other biblical texts that call for killing both in capital punishment and war. Cytron lists three arguments used by some in Judaism to support capital punishment based on biblical evidence. They are "moral order demands it" [capital punishment] (Num 35:33); retribution as in the the "life for a life" statement "(Deut 19:21) restores balance; capital punishment fosters deterrence (no text cited).[39] Cytron concludes: "There can be no misreading, then, of the Bible. On the one hand, it says 'Don't kill,' but then it goes on to sanction the state to do it."[40] The rabbis, however, "composed their own legal and midrashic responses, nearly all of which effectively removed the death penalty from use in that society."[41] Shalom Albeck regards Exod 20:13 as not a "practical instruction directing one how to act," because killing is mandated elsewhere in the Bible, but a "principle which gives its special quality to the concept of the sanctity of life."[42] He also notes the lengths to which rabbis went to avoid sanctioning killing even under legal circumstances.[43]

David Noel Freedman, Jeffrey C. Geoghegan, and Michael M. Homon subscribe to the "murder" translation, quoting Deut 4:42 as "whoever *murders* his neighbor unintentionally and did not hate him in times before."[44] They moreover state that the commandment only applies to "personal relations between Israelites, as the killing of Israel's enemies in war is almost always a commendable action, including, at times, women and children, though this is much rarer."[45] Mining Joshua, Judges, and Samuel for examples, they conclude that "a violation of the commandment prohibiting murder would need to meet the following criteria: the victim must not be an Israelite enemy, the death cannot be the result of

---

[39] Rabbi Barry D. Cytron, "Social Justice in a World of Injustices," *Proceedings of the Center for Jewish-Christian Leaning: Jews and Christians Speak of the Ten Commandments* (St. Paul, MN: University of St. Thomas, 1996) 57.

[40] Ibid.

[41] Ibid.

[42] Shalom Albeck, "The Essence of Religious Faith," in Segal, ed., *The Ten Commandments in History and Tradition*, 282.

[43] Ibid. 282–83.

[44] David Noel Freedman, with Jeffrey C. Geoghegan and Michael M. Homon, *The Nine Commandments: Uncovering a Hidden Pattern of Crime and Punishment in the Hebrew Bible* (New York: Doubleday, 2000) 111. *Erratum:* This paragraph belongs on page 59 prior to "The mainline traditions. . . ."

[45] Ibid. 112.

suicide (assisted or self-inflicted), or capital punishment, and the murder must not result from self-defense, the defense of others, or an accident."[46]

Gerald J. Blidstein discusses the use of the word *rtsh* in the Bible and Rabbinic texts in a 1965 article that appeared in the journal *Judaism*.[47] He argues effectively that not only does "kill" best represent the biblical word, but that understanding carried over into "Talmudic times."[48] He notes that discussions of capital punishment in the Mekhilta and the Jerusalem Talmud (*Sanh.* 4:6) use the word *rtsh* to describe the deed of both the court and the murderer.[49] The word is also used in the broader sense of "kill" in *She'iltot* (Vayechi, no. 34), *Midrash Hagadol, Zohar, Hilchot Rozeach, Sefer Ha-mizvoth*.[50] He points out that Moses Maimonides (the twelfth-century Spanish scholar) understood the word *rtsh* to apply "to killing in general,"[51] as did Isaac Abarbanel (a fifteenth-century Portuguese biblical scholar).[52] Moreover, he adds that Isaac Leeser, the American, in his early English translation for Jews (1855), used the word "kill" for the sixth commandment.[53] Blidstein concludes that "Biblical usage does not limit *rezichah*[54] to murder, rather extending it to describe all killing, even to that which is biblically ordained."[55]

Pointing out that the commandments are stated in second-person singular language, Moshe Weinfeld holds that each Israelite was obligated to obey them.[56] He writes, "The Decalogue is to be seen, then, as a basic list of concrete imperatives applicable to every individual Israelite. They represent a distillation, so to speak, of the core demands made by the God of Israel on those covenanted to him."[57] But this is not to say that they had a different status from other biblical directives. Weinfeld notes that there are other statements of moral principles that are at least as

---

[46] Ibid. 112–13.

[47] Gerald J. Blidstein. "Capital Punishment: The Classic Jewish Discussion," *Judaism* 14 (1965) 159–71.

[48] Ibid. 161.

[49] Ibid.

[50] Ibid. 162.

[51] Ibid.

[52] Ibid. 159.

[53] Ibid. 168, n. 1.

[54] A form of *rtsh*.

[55] Blidstein, "Capital Punishment," 162.

[56] Moshe Weinfeld, "The Uniqueness of the Decalogue," in Segal, ed., *The Ten Commandments in History and Tradition*, 11.

[57] Ibid.

significant in the Bible. "Love your neighbor" is an example.[58] Ephraim Urbach has an extended discussion of the place of the Ten Commandments in Jewish liturgy. He notes that the commandments were recited daily in Temple worship, according to the Mishnah, and perhaps also in synagogues.[59] Some Jewish communities practiced a regular recitation of the commandments during worship, but in other communities they were not regularly recited in order not to elevate them above other laws.[60] Urbach cites an explanation found in the Jerusalem Talmud as to why the Ten Commandments were not regularly read in some synagogues. The "Minim"[61] had made the heretical claim that only the Ten Words were spoken to the Israelites at Sinai.[62] Since most Jews during the period when the Talmud was being constructed believed that all of the Torah and not just the Ten Words was spoken at Sinai, a decision was made not to privilege them in such a way as to lead others to that conclusion. In other words, undue attention should not be given to the Ten Commandments because other instructions were given at Sinai and they are equally important. These other words were also given in the hearing of all the gathered Israelites. Urbach himself does not believe that this is the reason for the cessation of the regular recitation of the commandments in the Jewish liturgy.

For over two thousand years Jews, as a people, were stateless and therefore not in positions of political power. The rabbis could write theoretically about what should be done or might be done, but most killing decisions were out of their hands. With the creation of the state of Israel, the Jewish religion was in the same position that the Catholic Church and some Protestant denominations were in earlier as state-favored churches. Israel readily adopted a no-capital-punishment policy for ordinary criminal offenses, but it obviously has not divested itself of war or

---

[58] Ibid.

[59] Ephraim E. Urbach, "The Decalogue in Jewish Worship," in Segal, ed., *The Ten Commandments in History and Tradition*, 162–63.

[60] Ibid. 161–89.

[61] The identity of the Minim is unclear. Some have suggested that they were Christians or early Jewish Christians because later the word is used to refer to Christians. What can be said for sure is that the Minim held an alternate view on the recitation of the commandments and their relation to other laws. Geza Vermes thinks that they represented a "progressive, enlightened and intellectual *élite*" of Judaism in the Mediterranean world. See Geza Vermes, "The Decalogue and the Minim," in Matthew Black and Georg Fohrer, eds., *In Memoriam Paul Kahle*. BZAW 103 (Berlin: A. Töpelmann, 1968) 232–40, at 240.

[62] Urbach, "The Decalogue in Jewish Worship," 169.

violent means of self-defense. Whether they are regularly recited in worship or not, most Jews who attend synagogue are familiar with the commandments and understand them to be one of the pillars that undergird Jewish understandings of ethical behavior, lifestyle, and belief.

Chapter 5

The Fifth Commandment
in Roman Catholicism[1]

The Roman Catholic translations of the Bible during the second half of the twentieth century have bucked the trend to change the wording of Exod 20:13 from "kill" to "murder," reflecting both the hold of tradition in the Catholic Church and a broadening of the scope of the commandment, given changing thinking in the contemporary context. The Catholic Church never adopted the *sola scriptura* (scripture alone) of the Protestants, but maintained that interpretive authority in the church resides in a trinity of Scripture, tradition, and the magisterium (the pope and bishops).

The Interpretation of Scripture
in Roman Catholicism

The Roman Catholic Church teaches that the authors of the Holy Scriptures were divinely inspired. The catechism distinguishes between Christianity as a "religion of the book" and a "religion of the Word."[2] Christianity, it explains, is not the former, but the latter. "The Word" with a capital W refers to Christ. This means that all of Scripture is to be interpreted through the teachings of Christ and the Christ event itself (Jesus'

---

[1] The "You shall not kill" commandment is the fifth commandment in Roman Catholicism.

[2] *The Catechism of the Catholic Church* (2nd ed. Washington, D.C.: United States Catholic Conference, 1997) Part One, Article 3:II, 108.

71

life, crucifixion, and resurrection). Therefore Exod 20:13 is interpreted in light of the sayings of Jesus in the New Testament, particularly Matt 5:21-22, where the commandment is actually quoted. The catechism further says that Scripture is to be studied for both its literal and spiritual meanings.[3] Catholic interpretations, therefore, are concerned with killing both in its literal and spiritual forms, and this is clear in the extended discussion of the commandment in the catechism.

The Ten Commandments fall under the category of what is "obligatory for Christians."[4] They are to be understood in the context of covenant because they were first revealed as part of the covenant at Sinai. This means that those who have covenanted with God, whether Jews or Christians, keep the commandments as part of their responsibilities as covenant partners. Nevertheless, the catechism states, these precepts can also be accessed through reason alone.[5] Therefore all people should be able to grasp the essential rightness of what is being communicated.

Pacifism in the Early Church and the Movement toward Sanctioning Killing

Early Christians appear to have been pacifists. Church historians tell us that there are few accounts of Christians in the military in the early years of the church.[6] However, soldiers were converted while in the military. One early source reads: "A soldier of the lower ranks shall kill no one. If ordered to do so, he shall not obey, and he shall not take an oath."[7] Higher-ranking personnel who were in a position to order others to kill were advised to resign.[8] Christians expected the imminent return of Christ and were therefore reluctant to become involved in worldly affairs. They were opposed to taking loyalty oaths to the emperor (a requirement for those serving in the military) because such oaths required a nod to pagan belief. Moreover, they took the words of Jesus seriously: "You

---

[3] *The Catechism of the Catholic Church* (2nd ed. Washington, DC: United States Catholic Conference, 1997) Part 1, art. 3, nos. 106, 108, 129, 116, 117 (pp. 31, 36, 33).

[4] *The Catechism* (1997) Part 3, Section 2, ch. 2, no. 2068 (p. 502).

[5] *The Catechism* (1997) Part 3, Section 2, ch. 2, nos. 2060–2062.

[6] Guy F. Hershberger, *War, Peace and Nonresistance* (Scottsdale, PA: Herald Press, 1953) 65–70.

[7] Louis J. Swift, *The Early Fathers on War and Military Service* (Wilmington: Michael Glazier, 1983) 47.

[8] Ibid.

have heard that it was said to your ancestors, 'You shall not kill, and whoever kills will be liable to judgment.' But I say to you, whoever is angry with his brother shall be liable to judgment. . . ."[9] Historian Guy Hershberger quotes the third-century bishop of Carthage, Cyrian, as saying that Christians "are not allowed to kill, but they must be ready to be put to death themselves."[10] According to James Megivern, in the early fourth century Lucius Lactantius argued that the prohibition against killing precisely refers to what "men regard as ethical."[11] He declared that "killing itself is prohibited"[12] by the commandment. This is consistent with much of early Christian teaching until the emperor Constantine made Christianity a state religion, thereby forcing the church to become involved in the messy and sometimes violent business of state. By the late fourth century a section of the Canons of Hippolytus read: "A Christian should not voluntarily become a soldier unless compelled to by someone in authority. He should have a sword, but he should not be commanded to shed blood."[13] In the same century Basil of Caesarea permitted killing in war under some circumstances, but as penance the killer had to "abstain from communion for three years."[14] Clearly, Christians were struggling with the issue.

The church developed "just war" theory in order to theologically cope with the incongruity between biblical teachings (particularly New Testament teachings) and the desire of the state to wage war. Wars that were declared to be just, however, tended to be wars the state wanted to fight. The church provided the justification needed for capital punishment, judging it permissible when it serves to protect the innocent, to keep society safe, and to satisfy the desire of the state (and sometimes the church itself) to get rid of troublesome people.

The Roman Catholic Church has a long history as a state church in European and Latin American contexts. The Vatican itself was divorced from the state of Italy only in 1929. That divorce in many ways freed the church to be itself without the entanglements of secular politics. During

---

[9] Matthew 5:21-22b, *New American Bible.*

[10] Hershberger, *War, Peace and Nonresistance,* 68, quoting the Epistles of Cyprian, 1:6, in Alexander Roberts and James Donaldson, eds., *The Ante-Nicene Fathers,* 10 vols. (New York: Charles Scribner's Sons, 1908–1913) 5:277.

[11] James J. Megivern, *The Death Penalty: An Historical and Theological Survey* (New York: Paulist, 1997) 26.

[12] Ibid.

[13] Swift, *The Early Fathers on War and Military Service,* 93.

[14] Ibid. 94.

the twentieth century the Catholic Church softened its views on particular issues such as capital punishment and war in ways that affected its reading of the "You shall not kill" commandment.

Consistency in Translation

The official translation of the Roman Catholic Church for many centuries was the Latin Vulgate.[15] Jerome made this official translation from Greek and Hebrew into Latin in the fourth century. The Vulgate translated the fifth commandment into the Latin phrase *"non occides."*[16] The verb means kill or slaughter. The noun form of the word means "wholesale slaughter or destruction, extermination, massacre."[17] The Latin word chosen clearly has in mind killing that takes place beyond a one-on-one crime in a back alley.

The first English translation of the Pentateuch in Roman Catholic circles is known as the Douay (1609) because it was translated in Douay, Flanders (Belgium). The Latin Vulgate was the source text of the Douay, not the original-language texts. The fifth commandment was translated into English as "Thou shalt not kill." The Douay was updated several times over the course of the centuries. Francis Kenrick, who became archbishop of Baltimore, undertook a revision of the Douay for American Catholics in 1842.[18] Kenrick, who knew Hebrew, completed his Pentateuch translation in 1860. He translated "kill," but added a note explaining that the commandment excluded self-defense or "the just exercise of public authority. . . ."[19] He did not give a reason for the exception. However, a note attached to the parallel text in Deut 5:17 quotes Augustine as excluding war and capital punishment from the scope of the commandment.[20] The *Jerusalem Bible,* published in 1966, the *New Jerusalem Bible,* published in 1985, and the *New American Bible,* first published in 1970, all translated "kill." The last of the three was a fresh translation from the

---

[15] Vulgate means common, as in the common language of the Latin-speaking people of the time.

[16] *Biblia Sacra Vulgata* (Stuttgart: Deutsche Bibelgesellschaft, 1994) 104.

[17] P.G.W. Glare, ed., *Oxford Latin Dictionary* (Oxford: Clarendon Press, 1982) 1232.

[18] Gerald P. Fogarty, s.j., "American Catholic Translations of the Bible," in Ernest S. Frerichs, ed., *The Bible and Bibles in America* (Atlanta: Scholars, 1988) 120.

[19] Francis Patrick Kenrick, *The Pentateuch* (Baltimore: Kelly, Hedian & Piet, 1860) 228, n. 17.

[20] Ibid. 485, n. 15.

original languages by (mostly) Catholic scholars. In sum, all of the English translations produced in the Roman Catholic tradition have been consistent in the translation of the commandment.

What the Catechism Says

In its official catechism the Roman Catholic Church has a long and detailed discussion of this commandment. It specifies not only what constitutes a violation of the commandment, but what the commandment requires. The catechism opens by affirming the sacredness of human life. It says that "no one can . . . claim . . . the right . . . to destroy an innocent human being."[21] "The deliberate murder of an innocent person is gravely contrary to the dignity of the human being, to the golden rule, and to the holiness of the Creator."[22] The key word in this injunction is "innocent," but the catechism does not explain what it means by "innocent" or why the commandment would be limited to innocent human beings. It does say, quoting a papal document: "Nothing and no one can in any way permit the killing of an innocent human being, whether a fetus or an embryo, an infant or an adult, or an old person, or one suffering from an incurable disease or a person who is dying."[23]

The catechism permits killing to defend oneself or to protect others for whom one is responsible (on a personal, family, or state level). Such killing is not only appropriate but "a grave duty."[24] In support of this the catechism appeals to Thomas Aquinas (thirteenth century), who outlined principles of just war.[25] Public protection includes capital punishment and war, though the catechism suggests that if "bloodless" means can "defend human lives . . . protect the public order and the safety of persons," those means are preferable to executing someone or engaging in warfare.[26]

[21] *The Catechism* (1997) Part 3, Section 2, ch. 2, art. 5, 2258.

[22] Ibid. 2261.

[23] John Paul II, *Evangelium Vitae* 57, quoting *Iura et Bona* (May 5, 1980) II: *AAS* 72 (1980) 546.

[24] *The Catechism* (1997) Part 3, Section 2, ch. 2, art. 5, 2263–64.

[25] Aquinas listed three rules of just war: a ruler with legitimate authority may wage war but not a private individual; there must be a just cause; the intent must be to "achieve some good or avoid some evil." Paul E. Sigmund, ed. and trans., *St. Thomas Aquinas on Politics and Ethics* (New York: W. W. Norton & Co., 1988) 64–65.

[26] *The Catechism* (1997) Part 3, Section 2, ch. 2, art. 5, 2266.

Under this commandment many issues that are directly related to killing are discussed and prohibited including intentional homicide, abortion, euthanasia, and suicide. In addition to these are violations that may lead to "spiritual death," such as scandal. "Abuse of food, alcohol, tobacco, medicine" or causing accidents by excessive speed are also condemned.[27] Other issues considered under the "You shall not kill" commandment include the use of human beings in scientific experimentation, "kidnapping and hostage taking . . . terrorism," anger and hatred, treatment of corpses, and the just war theory.[28] Like other sensitive traditions, this one recognizes that death can take many forms: spiritual, psychological, or physical.

The catechism is resigned to the use of warfare for a nation's self-defense. It does not prohibit war, but it limits it in the traditional way by applying the ethical standards of just war. In order to be just, a war must have a just cause (usually self-defense) and be fought in a just manner (the innocent are protected; only enough force is used to accomplish the goal, etc.). The catechism assigns the duty of determining whether a war meets the just war criteria to "those who have responsibility for the common good," not the church.[29]

Catholic Voices

In the early twentieth century, when the industrial revolution was taking its toll, Catholics, like their socially conscious counterparts in other faith traditions, in sermons, commentaries, and popular articles applied the commandment to abuse of workers, adulteration of milk, preventable accidents, poor housing, alcohol abuse, and diseased meat.[30]

In a series of lectures delivered in 1936, Patrick Joseph Gannon noted that some have become vegetarians in response to this commandment, believing that even the slaying of animals is prohibited. He writes of such persons that "as long as they confine themselves to making this a counsel of perfection, no harm is done."[31] The notion of a "counsel of

[27] *The Catechism,* Part 3, Section 2, ch. 2, art. 5, 2284, 2290.

[28] Ibid. 2292–2296, 2297, 2302–2303, 2299, 2309.

[29] Ibid. 2309.

[30] J. V. Schubert, *The Commandments of God and Their Practical Application in Daily Life* (New York: Joseph F. Wagner, ©1916).

[31] Patrick Joseph Gannon, *The Old Law and the New Morality* (London: Burns, Oates & Washbourne, 1937) 64.

perfection" is derived from the words of Jesus as found in Matt 19:21, where Jesus suggests that the wealthy young man sell all that he has and give it to the poor—if he wants to be perfect. The Catholic Church formerly taught that among laity, priests, and religious only the last were held to a higher standard of piety that included the disciplines of what are popularly called poverty, chastity, and obedience. Vatican II clarified that everyone is to strive for holiness and perfection. There is no distinction in this between religious and laity.[32] Notice that the fifth commandment does not have a direct object attached to it. What is it that you shall not kill? The question of whether or not humans are meant to be the sole object has been raised in each of the four broad traditions. Needless to say, few have extended "You shall not kill" to include animals. The Hebrew word *rtsh*, found in Exod 20:13, is used elsewhere in the Bible to describe killing *by* an animal, but not killing of an animal by a human being.

In the late twentieth century leading Roman Catholic clergy began expressing increasingly pacifistic views on the issue of killing. Pope John Paul II took a strong stance against capital punishment, arguing that it is no longer necessary as a means of providing for public safety or punishment. He issued an encyclical in 1995 stating emphatically that developments in penal systems should make capital punishment unnecessary.[33] Michael O'Connell, following Joseph Cardinal Bernardin, writes that "one cannot be against abortion and for capital punishment and have a consistent ethic of life."[34] Bernardin traced the evolving ethic of the Roman Catholic Church in relation to issues of war, capital punishment, and other life-threatening events.[35] He did not speak directly to the "do not kill" commandment, but noted that "the sense that every human life has transcendent value has led a whole stream of the Christian tradition to argue that life may never be taken. That position is held by an increasing number of Catholics. . . ."[36] Michaël Devaux declares: "The legislation of this proscription has as wide a scope as we can imagine. It

[32] Telephone interview with Fr. Frank Bryan of Marian College, Indianapolis, Sept. 3, 2004.

[33] John Paul II, *Evangelium Vitae* 56 (March 25, 1995), from the Vatican website, http://www.vatican.va/edocs/ENG0141/_PP.HTML.

[34] Michael J. O'Connell, "Social Justice in a World of Injustices: A Christian Perspective," *Proceedings of the Center for Jewish-Christian Leaning: Jews and Christians Speak of the Ten Commandments* (St. Paul, MN: University of St. Thomas, 1996) 62.

[35] Joseph Cardinal Bernardin, "Cardinal Bernardin's Call for a Consistent Ethic of Life," *Origins* 13, no. 29 (Dec. 29, 1983) 491–94.

[36] Ibid. 492.

includes everyone. No one has the right to kill. . . . It does not suffer us to place conditions upon it. No situation can justify murder."[37] The interchangeability of the words kill and murder in this statement muddies the waters. Is killing prohibited, or only murder?

In recent years the Roman Catholic Church has also begun to speak out against nuclear war and other forms of mass destruction that do not allow for the protection of the innocent.

The Roman Catholic Church has been fairly consistent in its translation and interpretation of the "you shall not kill" commandment throughout the twentieth century and into the twenty-first century. In its thinking, the commandment was never meant to be understood as absolute. There is still room for killing for self-defense or defense of others by the state or individuals, though bloodless means of achieving an objective are to be preferred.

[37] Michaël Devaux, "The Truth of Love, the Lie of Death," *Communio: International Catholic Review* 23 (1996) 110–21, at 111.

Chapter 6

When "You shall not kill" Became "You shall not murder"

Context: As I write these words I am sitting in my study, waiting for the chapel bells to ring. The ringing of the bells signals that the funeral cortege of the second police officer killed in Indianapolis in five weeks will pass by the seminary. We will all go outside to line the streets and pay our last respects. The shooting of the officer was a shock to all of us. This is a quiet middle-class campus community. He was a member of a college police force expecting to deal with no more than an unruly or intoxicated student. He had asked the man to leave the campus. The man pulled the officer's gun and shot him dead with a single bullet. The police caught up with the perpetrator later that day and shot him dead on a sidewalk, a few blocks from the governor's mansion. The police officer was thirty-one years old. The killer was twenty-four. He had a history of mental illness.

I do not live in an ivory tower. I walk the same streets as everyone else. I fear the same fears as everyone else. But killing is not the solution to the problem of killing. In the late twentieth century and into the twenty-first century there was a movement away from the traditional wording of the sixth commandment, from "You shall not kill" to the more limited "You shall not murder." This would be appropriate if it more accurately reflected the meaning of the biblical text, but it does not. The word "murder" conjures up images of a lone, lawless individual killing an innocent victim. The new threat to human life, terrorism, is rightly placed under the category of murder. However, the vast majority of violent and unnatural deaths during the last century were not the result of murder, but actions that in English are covered by the word "kill." Limiting the scope of the commandment to illegal one-on-one killing exempts the primary causes of unnatural deaths in the twentieth and early twenty-first centuries: war, capital punishment, government policies of starvation or government sponsored terrorism, lack of health-care and hygienic programs (clean water, clean air, absence of toxins in the environment), and preventable accidents and diseases that kill far more people.

In democracies, adults have voice and vote that shape the direction their government takes. The government is not an entity outside of the governed, but an expression of its will. This book is not arguing that governments need to conform to religious law. It assumes that govern-ments must be secular and democratic in order to serve the needs of all of their citizens. In the United States the responsibilities of government are outlined in the Constitution and its accompanying amendments, and on the state and local level by their respective constitutions and statutes. Fortunately, in a democracy, citizens have not only a say in the actions that governments take but a responsibility to actively enter the political process for their own sake and for the sake of those who are most vul-nerable: children, the poor, the foreigner, minority groups, the elderly, the infirm, etc. In the United States the majority of citizens, as individ-uals, are members of or participants in churches and synagogues that claim to be guided by insights gleaned from the Bible. Bible translators and interpreters, like nuclear physicists, bear a portion of the responsi-bility for how others use what they have produced. When "You shall not kill" became "You shall not murder," translators set a new ethical direc-tion and sanctioned all kinds of killing that fall outside of the narrow definition of murder. If the word clearly meant murder in the Hebrew, it would have been appropriate to make the change. But when there is doubt, it is inappropriate to go with the more lethal reading.

During the first half of the twentieth century an expansive semantic range was given to "You shall not kill" by sensitive interpreters who recognized the social, spiritual, and political dimensions of the com-mandment in their context. By the end of the century translators had narrowed the semantic possibilities by limiting the prohibition to murder, a word that in English usage is narrowly defined and problematic precisely because it is a legal term. As such, the meaning of the word varies with legal jurisdictions.[1] The problem with the choice of the word "murder"

---

[1] See Chapter One above for a comparison of different state definitions of murder.

as a translation of the Hebrew word *rtsh* is that unlike "kill," "murder" is a legal term that is defined differently in different places.

Murder is relatively rare. It was probably even rarer when individuals did not have the ability to instantly end the life of another through the use of a gun or weapons of mass destruction. Most crimes of murder are crimes of passion or, in contemporary society, drug-related. In 2003 there were eighty-one homicides in Indianapolis, a city with a population of 806,454 according to the U.S. Census for the year 2000. This means that at least 806,373 people managed to get through the entire year without killing anyone. Moreover, the homicide rate includes accidental killings, police actions, (mostly) crimes of passion (by which I mean not only crossed lovers, but spur-of-the-moment actions committed in the heat of anger or in the course of committing another crime), and drug-related killings. Prohibiting murder is not an effective means of restraining people who engage in this crime, because statistically the persons committing the crimes are not constrained by an ethical code or they are acting out of passion and not logic or morals. Such individuals may be constrained, but not by the use of a commandment. It is unlikely that the commandment was given to stop people from doing what they normally do not do anyway.

Killing, outside of murder, is also not something that most normal people engage in. So why is "kill" the better term? Many more adults are complicit in killing than murder because they have a voice in community-wide, statewide, or national decisions to use capital punishment, war, or other types of killing as a means of solving problems. We all have a voice in decisions about healthcare and public safety. As the other commandments that list prohibitions include behaviors that people really do—covet, commit adultery, steal, and lie—it is likely that this commandment is also meant to cover what people really do.

No doubt events in the twentieth and twenty-first centuries—two world wars, Vietnam, the Killing Fields of Cambodia, the Cultural Revolution in China, Stalinism, the Armenian massacre, the slaughter of the Jews, Pearl Harbor, Rwanda and Darfur, the atomic bombing of Nagasaki and Hiroshima, the wars and exploitation in the Congo, the attack on the World Trade Center, terrorism, and other atrocities—influenced the translators of this biblical text. Of course, many people do believe that killing has a place in the maintenance of law and order and that the killing of some will prevent the massacre of thousands or even millions of innocent people (as in the use of atomic weapons). Therefore they think it is appropriate that killing be permitted by legal authorities.

The death penalty, they may argue, not only gets rid of the immediate problem but functions as a deterrent to others contemplating similar crimes. But this has not been proven to be the case. States that have a death penalty do not have fewer capital crimes. Moreover, statistics show that the death penalty is disproportionately assigned to racial and ethnic minorities (particularly African-Americans), indicating that there is an agenda beyond safety that drives this sentence. Non-lethal means such as imprisonment can be an effective way to keep the public safe, with the added benefit of allowing the offender to amend for crimes committed and do some good as well. Society really cannot afford to lose people who have the ability to make a contribution, and in some cases a unique contribution, to society.

Wars employ or conscript the young and the poor who have few options other than to be soldiers. Those calling for war live in their protected bubbles, leading from behind and making sure that their children are never placed in harm's way. This is significantly different from the biblical wars, where those calling for the war—Joshua, Saul (with his sons and heirs), David, and Ahab—were all on the battlefield. Because of the nature of modern warfare, those killed in war are not primarily other soldiers but civilians and those who just happen to be in the way ("collateral damage"). The destruction of infrastructure, including water purification systems and food and medical delivery systems, causes the death of the most vulnerable: children and the infirm first. This would appear to violate even just war criteria, let alone the "You shall not kill" commandment.

Murder itself, of course, is a kind of killing that is included in the more general term "kill." Murder rates can be brought down, as has been demonstrated in a number of cities in the United States and other countries. Citizens who want to bring down the murder rate can support policies and programs that identify at-risk youth and nurture them away from violent behavior. They can support gun control. They can vote in favor of additional funding to train police in non-lethal methods of conflict control so that the lives of both the police and the perpetrators may be spared. Of course, persons who unlawfully kill must be held accountable. Terrorists are not likely to be constrained by a translation of "you shall not kill," since their purpose is to kill and thereby create fear and chaos. The world community needs to work on this issue collectively.

The Ten Commandments have served the synagogue and church well for the past two thousand years. To be sure, their wisdom was too often not heeded or incorporated into the lives of individuals or the community. But they were there, and from time to time they were dusted off, reread, and reconsidered. The Ten Commandments function well as a pedagogical tool. They are easy to memorize and therefore easy carry along life's journey. When "you shall not kill" became "you shall not murder," the prohibition against killing was removed not just from the text and common conversation, but increasingly from memory itself, as young people growing up in the churches and synagogues are presented only one limited interpretation of the commandment. Some may argue that a moral stance against killing in a broader sense may be arrived at by a sophisticated analysis of biblical texts in their broader context. But what ancient people knew and we need to relearn is that the average person is not going to wade through a sophisticated and complicated interpretive defense of a particular line of argument. Walter Harrelson once told me that we are all complicit in wars and other policies that end human life prematurely, but happily we are also all complicit in actions that enhance and protect life. Those of us who do have a say can work to increase the latter and decrease the former.

In spite of the lack of new knowledge about the word *rtsḥ*, of new discoveries in the Dead Sea Scrolls or new insights into syntactical or grammatical functions in ancient Hebrew, at the end of the twentieth century scholars began changing the translation of the word רצח from "kill" to "murder." Will changing the translation back to the original and more accurate word cause people to stop killing each other? Will it bring in an era of peace? One thing that it *will* do is cause those who look to the Bible for guidance to pause, to continue the conversation, and examine issues related to killing. Perhaps we can creatively develop more ways to solve problems without resorting to violent and lethal means that foreshorten the lives of so many. The "murder" translation, on the other hand, truncates that discussion and gives permission for unspeakable evil to continue.

Appendix 1

List of Bibles Reading "kill" and "murder"

P = Protestant   RC = Roman Catholic   J = Jewish

KILL

1395	Wyclif (spelled "sle") (P)
1530	Tyndale Pentateuch (P)
1535	Coverdale (P)
1560	Geneva (P)
1568	Bishops' Bible (P)
1609	Douay (RC)
1611	*Authorized Version* ("King James Version")[1] (P)
1749–1752	Richard Challoner (RC)
1853	Isaac Leeser (J)
1856	Samuel Sharpe (P)
1860	Francis Patrick Kenrick (RC)
1890	John Nelson Darby (P)
1901	*American Standard* (P)
1952	*Revised Standard Version* (P)
1970	*Jerusalem Bible* (RC)
1970	*New American Bible* (RC)

[1] The popular *Scofield Bible* retains the KJV. In 1917 there was no note on Exod 20:13. In 1967 the *New Scofield* in a note indicated that "kill" meant "murder."

| 1985 | *New Jerusalem Bible* (RC) |
| 1994 | *Twenty-First Century King James Version* (P) |

MURDER

1885	*English Revised* (P)
1898	*Young's Literal Translation* (Robert Young) (P)
1917	*The Torah*, JPS (J)
1922	*The Complete Bible in Modern English* (P)
1931	*The Bible: An American Translation* (P)
1935	Moffat (P)
1959	*Amplified* (P)
1960?	*New American Standard Bible* (P)
1962	*The Torah* (later incorporated into the *TANAKH*, 1985) (J)
1973	*New International Version* (P)
1981	*The Living Torah* (Aryeh Kaplan) (J)
1982	*New King James Version* (P)
1983	*The Five Books of Moses* (Everett Fox) (J)
1989	*New Revised Standard Version* (note reads "or kill)" (P)
1995	*Contemporary English* (P)
1996	*New Living Translation* (P)
2001	*English Standard Version* (Note adds "The Hebrew word also covers causing human death through carelessness or negligence.") (P)
2004	*Holman Christian Standard Bible* (P)

Appendix 2

A Study of the Word רצח

The following texts indicate that רצח in its biblical usage extended beyond the idea of "murder," which in English and American law, as well as colloquial use, is not an adequate translation of the Hebrew word used in Exod 20:13. All translations in this appendix are mine unless otherwise indicated.[1] Hebrew phrases are taken from *Biblia Hebraica Stuttgartensia* less the nikud.

The Meaning of רצח Is Sometimes Ambiguous

The word רצח appears four times in lists where the behavior indicated by the use of the verb is prohibited (the nature of what is not to be done is ambiguous). This is true in the following texts:

Exodus 20:13 and Deuteronomy 5:17, לא תרצח, "You shall not kill."

Jeremiah 7:9, הגנב רצח ונאף, "Will you steal, kill, and commit adultery . . .?"

Hosea 4:2, אלה וכחש ורצח וגנב ונאף, "swearing, deceiving, killing, stealing, committing adultery. . . ."

---

[1] Words that appear in brackets do not appear in the text. They substitute for "he," "him," and "his" in order to create an inclusive-language translation.

When רצח (*rtsh*) appears in a list, as in the four examples above, it is impossible to form a precise definition of what it means (murder? kill? as in suicide? killing in war? capital punishment? police action? human sacrifice?). The reader only knows that the action is prohibited. Four out of thirteen appearances of this word in verbal form are in such ambiguous lists.

רצח (*rtsh*) and the Cities of Refuge

The word רצח is found frequently in the texts that describe the "cities of refuge" in Numbers 35 and Deuteronomy 4. Chapter 35 of the book of Numbers has an extended discussion of killings of various kinds, and of appropriate and inappropriate revenge. The word רצח in its noun/ participle form, רוצח, is used frequently.

Deuteronomy 4:41-42

אז יבדיל משה שלש ערים בעבר הירדן מזרחה שמש
לנס שמה רוצח אשר ירצח את רעהו בבלי דעת
והוא לא שנא לו מתמול שלשום ונס אל אחת מן הערים האל וחי:

> Then Moses set apart three cities, when crossing the Jordan, from the east, for a רוצח that ירצח a friend without knowing to flee to when [the killer] had not been a hater of [the deceased] in the past. [The killer] will flee to one of the cities of God and live.

This is the only place in the Hebrew Bible where a רוצח (m.s. participle) "killer" is actually said to kill ירצח (3 m.s. imperfect/prefix) using the same verbal root. This is odd, given the frequent use of noun and verb forms of the same root in Hebrew in sentences. In Deut 4:41-42 רצח clearly refers to an unintentional killing, not murder.

Numbers 35, Legal Killing by a גאל

In Numbers 35 the noun form of killer, רוצח, is used eighteen times. The verbal form of רוצח, רצח, appears twice (35:27, 30). Ironically, it is used to describe the action of the גאל who happens upon the רוצח outside the boundaries of the city of refuge, and to describe the action a court may take against a person who has killed another. Neither of these is considered murder. Both are within the bounds of killing that is legal.

Numbers 35:27

וּמָצָא אֹתוֹ גֹּאֵל הַדָּם מִחוּץ לִגְבוּל עִיר מִקְלָטוֹ וְרָצַח גֹּאֵל הַדָּם אֶת
הָרֹצֵחַ אֵין לוֹ דָּם

> And the redeemer of blood finds [the killer] outside the boundary of
> the city of refuge and the redeemer of blood kills the killer, there is
> no blood[guilt] to [the redeemer].

The רוצח is protected only within the boundaries of the cities of refuge. This is the first place in Numbers 35 where the verb רצח is used (except for the participle) and it describes the killing of the רוצח by the גואל when the רוצח is found outside the boundaries of the city of refuge. In this text the word רצח (3 m.s. perfect/affix in a vav reversive construction) does not mean murder, because the גואל is not guilty of a crime: "there is no blood to him." This is not an illegal killing, murder.

The Use of the Term רצח in the Administration of Justice

Numbers 35:30

כֹּל מַכֵּה נֶפֶשׁ לְפִי עֵדִים יִרְצַח אֶת הָרֹצֵחַ וְעֵד אֶחָד לֹא יַעֲנֶה
בְנֶפֶשׁ לָמוּת

> Everyone who cuts down a life according to witnesses, [someone]
> will kill the killer, but a single witness will not cause a person to die.

In this verse the deed of the court is ירצח (3 m.s. imperfect/prefix). It does not mean murder in these verses because it is done legally within the court system.

Unexpected Use of the Word רצח

1 Kings 21:19a, b

וְדִבַּרְתָּ אֵלָיו לֵאמֹר כֹּה אָמַר יְהוָה הֲרָצַחְתָּ וְגַם יָרָשְׁתָּ

> You will speak to him saying: "Thus says YHWH: Have you killed and
> also possessed?"

The word appears in an interrogative phrase, הרצחת (hê plus 2 m.s. perfect/affix) directed to Ahab. The meaning of the word is uncertain. Ahab has not killed anyone in this context.

רצח Cannot Mean Murder In This Text

Proverbs 22:13

אמר עצל ארי בחוץ בתוך רחבות ארצח

> An idle person says, "a lion is outside. I will be killed in the middle of the street."

In this verse the word appears as a first common singular niphal imperfect (prefix). Even if the imagined lion does appear, attack, and kill the person, it is not murder because the lion is incapable of making moral decisions.

Texts That Are Unclear In Their Use of the Word רצח

Psalm 62:4 [English 62:3]

עד אנה תהותתו על איש תרצחו כלכם כקיר נטוי גדר הדחויה

The meaning is unclear. It is telling that most of the translations *(NRSV, JPS, NIV, REB, NKJV)* that adopted the word "murder" for רצח *(rtsḥ)* in Exod 20:13 do not use that word in translating this verse. Frank-Lothar Hossfeld notes that the use of the piel (3 m.p. imperfect/prefix) in this verse indicates a "repeated, habitual action."[2]

רצח as Murder

Hosea 6:9

וכחכי איש גדודים חבר כהנים דרך ירצחו שכמה כי זמה עשו

> "Like a band of robbers, priests hide. They kill on the way to Shechem because they made a plan."

---

[2] Hossfeld, רצח, *TDOT* 13:634.

Killing after making a plan would seem to denote murder in light of the context of other unacceptable acts. This appears to be murder, if the planned killing is also illegal killing.[3] The verb appears in a 3 m.p. imperfect/prefix form.

Deuteronomy 22:26

וְלַנַּעַר לֹא תַעֲשֶׂה דָבָר אֵין לַנַּעַר חֵטְא מָוֶת כִּי כַּאֲשֶׁר יָקוּם אִישׁ עַל
רֵעֵהוּ וּרְצָחוֹ נֶפֶשׁ כֵּן הַדָּבָר הַזֶּה

> You will not do anything to the young woman. There is not a death-sin to the young woman because this is like when a person rises up against a neighbor and kills him. Thus is this thing.

In this verse, the word רצח (3 m.s. perfect/affix vav reversive) is used in a simile. The simile is used to support the innocence of the young woman. The man will die. The woman is not guilty. The use of the word in this text appears to be murder.

Psalm 94:6

אַלְמָנָה וְגֵר יַהֲרֹגוּ וִיתוֹמִים יְרַצֵּחוּ

> They kill widow and stranger, and they kill orphans.

In the context, the people doing this think that God will not know what is going on (v. 7). This suggests that widows, strangers, and orphans are being killed, but not in an outright way. They are killed through deprivation and neglect.[4] The verb appears in a 3 m.p. imperfect/prefix form.

In these three verses "murder" is perhaps the best translation of רצח: once in Ps 94:6, once in Hos 6:9, and once in Deut 22:26. Out of thirteen occurrences of the word רצח in the Hebrew Bible, it most likely means murder only three times.[5]

---

[3] See note attached to Psalm 62:4 in BHS.
[4] See note attached to Psalm 62:4 in BHS.
[5] For a technical discussion of the term see Hossfeld, רצח, *TDOT* 13:630–640.

Index of Subjects and Authors

Index of Biblical Citations